Gastric Sleeve Bariatric Bible 2022

800 Days Easy and Healthy Recipe Book with
A Complete Guide for Life Before and
After Bariatric Surgery

William Torres

Copyright© 2021By William TorresAll Rights Reserved

This book is copyright protected. It is only for personal use. You cannot amend, distribute, sell, use, quote or paraphrase any part of the content within this book, without the consent of the author or publisher.

Under no circumstances will any blame or legal responsibility be held against the publisher, or author, for any damages, reparation, or monetary loss due to the information contained within this book, either directly or indirectly.

Disclaimer Notice:

Please note the information contained within this document is for educational and entertainment purposes only. All effort has been executed to present accurate, up to date, reliable, complete information. No warranties of any kind are declared or implied. Readers acknowledge that the author is not engaged in the rendering of legal, financial, medical or professional advice. The content within this book has been derived from various sources. Please consult a licensed professional before attempting any techniques outlined in this book.

By reading this document, the reader agrees that under no circumstances is the author responsible for any losses, direct or indirect, that are incurred as a result of the use of the information contained within this document, including, but not limited to, errors, omissions, or inaccuracies.

CONTENT

Introduction 1

Chapter 1 All About Bariatric Surgery 2

Chapter 2 A New Way of Life 6

Chapter 3 Your Diet After Bariatric Surgery 10

Chapter 4 Full Liquid Foods 21

Chapter 5 Puréed Foods 27

Chapter 6 Soft Foods 34

Chapter 7 Breakfasts 42

Chapter 8 Soups and Stews 50

Chapter 9 Vegetables and Sides 57

Chapter 10 Poultry 64

Chapter 11 Pork, Beef and Lamb 71

Chapter 12 Fish and Seafood 78

Chapter 13 Desserts 86

Chapter 14 Staples, Sauces and Dressings 93

Appendix 1 Measurement Conversion Chart 99

Introduction

I have been invested in finding ways to successfully lose weight and keep it off since I can remember. Having struggled with my weight from a young age, I'm no stranger to yo-yo dieting. In my search for the perfect diet, I have come across various natural ways to lose weight—the Mediterranean diet being a firm favorite. But, the fact of the matter is not everyone can do this the natural way. Some people need help, and nothing presses the weight reset button as hard as bariatric surgery.

It's frequently someone's last desperate attempt to take their life and health back. Fortunately, the success rate of getting a gastric sleeve or bypass is high, so you get a second chance at life.

With that being said, surgery is not where this process ends. Weight-loss surgery is a life-changing procedure, which you will need to adapt to. You will have to change your relationship with food entirely. Gone are the days of using food as a method to celebrate achievements or suppress emotions. You won't be eating because you're bored or lonely, but to fuel your body efficiently.

The size of your new stomach will only be a fraction of what it used to be, and can only handle a small portion of food at a time. This makes what you put into your mouth extra important, and I want to help you feed your body with only the best, most delicious food available.

In this cookbook, I will walk you through the various types of bariatric surgery, but the focus will be on vertical sleeve gastrectomy since it is considered the safest yet still effective weight-loss surgery out of all four methods.

But what I'm most excited about is helping you navigate your new way of life, and assisting you in leaving behind any fear you might have surrounding bariatric surgery. I also can't wait to walk you through the bariatric transition diet and help you set up your kitchen to ensure long-term success.

Of course, what would a cookbook be without the cooking? I am proud of the selection of sleeve-friendly recipes that are included in this book. They're formatted to include the right balance of protein, carbohydrates, and fat. I've done all the math so you can just decide on the meal and prepare it knowing you'll experience no discomfort after. All meals are based on the bariatric diet and curated to exclude foods that upset your stomach.

I hope this cookbook will help you settle into life after weight-loss surgery with less anxiety while offering you some form of comfort (food) within the confines of the post-op diet.

Chapter 1 All About Bariatric Surgery

Bariatric surgical procedures are often the only hope for those that are severely obese. It works by inhibiting the amount of food a person can eat and limiting the calories they will consume per day. The fewer calories a person eats in relation to what their body needs to function, the more weight they will lose.

The most common weight-loss surgeries are gastric bypass, vertical sleeve gastrectomy (VSG), adjustable gastric band, and biliopancreatic diversion with duodenal switch (BPD/DS). All of these are done laparoscopically, which means they are minimally invasive, and the hospital stay won't be too long.

4 Types of Bariatric Procedures

Gastric Bypass (Roux-en-Y)

The first component of the procedure is separating the stomach into two sections. The small pouch connected to the esophagus will be approximately one ounce in volume and will continue to receive food. Food will no longer reach the bottom part of the stomach. Next, a section of the small intestine is disconnected and reconnected to the small part of the stomach. This means food will be re-routed directly from the stomach to the remaining intestine.

The procedure works on the same premise as most other weight-loss surgeries: the significant reduction of the stomach's size means only a small amount of food can be accommodated at a time, which translates to lower calorie intake. The fact that a part of the small intestine—which also absorbs calories—no longer has food going through it also decreases the absorption of nutrients and thus calories.

- The procedure is performed laparoscopically.
- Usually a three-day hospital stay.
- Two to four weeks of restricted activity post-op.
- Non-reversible.

Vertical Sleeve Gastrectomy

A VSG is where up to 80 percent of a person's stomach is removed by stapling and dividing it vertically. A banana-shaped section of the stomach remains. It works for the same reason that gastric bypass does—limited stomach capacity. A person isn't able to eat large portions, and this leads to reduced calorie intake.

In addition, VSG seems to affect gut hormones that play a role in hunger, satiety and stabilizing blood sugar levels (Ionut et al., 2013).

- The procedure is performed laparoscopically.
- Two-day hospital stay.
- Two to three weeks of restricted activity post-op.
- Non-reversible.
- Weight-loss results are similar to that of gastric bypass surgery, but the long-term maintenance of the weight loss is up to 50 percent higher (Richardson et al., 2009).

Adjustable Gastric Band

Often just called "the band," this procedure involves a silicone ring being placed around the top part of the stomach to create a small pouch. The size of the opening between the pouch and the more substantial part of the stomach can be adjusted. If the opening is big, the feeling of fullness after eating won't be nearly as much as when the opening is smaller.

To reduce the size of the opening, sterile saline is injected through a port placed under the person's skin. Similarly, the opening can be enlarged by withdrawing the liquid. This process is done gradually over time to achieve the ideal tightness.

The idea is that the band will restrict how much food can be eaten at any time combined with the slow speed at which it passes through the band leads to weight loss. However, some studies have challenged this notion, claiming that food passes through the band quickly, which means patients don't feel satiated for longer (Seeras et al., 2020).

- The procedure is done laparoscopically.
- Hospital stay is less than 24 hours.
- Involves no cutting or re-routing.
- Is reversible.
- Is the least effective of all the bariatric procedures.

Biliopancreatic Diversion with Duodenal Switch (BPD/DS)

The BPD/DS is similar to gastric bypass surgery except for two variances. The section of the small intestine that is bypassed is significantly larger. In addition, the food only mixes with the bile and pancreatic enzymes far down the small intestine resulting in minimal absorption of calories and nutrients.

It is usually done in two stages to minimize the risk of having a lengthy procedure. First, the doctor will do a VSG. Twelve to 18 months later, the bypass part of the process will be completed.

- The procedure is done either laparoscopically or as traditional open surgery.
- Hospital stay is up to three days.
- Non-reversible.
- A person will need to take vitamin and mineral supplements daily.
- Although it is the most effective of all bariatric surgeries, it is high risk and can cause long-term health problems.

Since the weight loss after the VSG part of the BPD/DS is so significant, doctors decided that sleeve gastrectomy is efficient enough to see results—with less risk and complications. Let's have a closer look at the advantages and disadvantages of the sleeve.

VSG Advantages

People who've had sleeve surgery lose up to 60-70% of excess weight.

Here is a breakdown of the common trend of weight loss:

- In the first two weeks, most people will lose around one pound a day. You can expect to drop anywhere from 10 to 20 pounds.
- In the first three months, expect a 35-45% reduction of weight.
- In the first six months, people lost up to 60% of any excess weight, and after a year, up to 70%.

This is impressive, considering that there's no need for foreign objects or re-routing of any kind.

But there are more advantages than just losing weight. You will also improve many weight-related health problems (Hoyuela, 2017).

These include:

- Type 2 diabetes
- Fatty liver disease
- Hypertension
- High cholesterol
- PCOS
- Infertility
- Sleep apnea
- And non-weight-related issues such as asthma, migraines, depression, and urinary incontinence.

VSG also removes the part of the stomach that produces Ghrelin—a hormone that stimulates hunger.

Then there's dumping syndrome—the discomfort so many bariatric patients experience when they overeat or consume sugary foods (Mayo Clinic, n.d.). Well, VSG is avoided or, at the very least, minimized since the opening of the stomach stays intact.

VSG Disadvantages

Compared to other bariatric surgeries, the drawbacks are minor. The main shortcoming is, strangely enough, one of the advantages—dumping syndrome. Since someone who has undergone VSG won't experience any discomfort after eating sugary foods, they'll be likely to continue consuming them. As you can imagine, this will significantly reduce any weight loss.

There's also a chance of gastric leaks and other complications related to stapling. As with other weight-loss surgery, the potential of vitamin deficiency exists, but can easily be overcome by drinking supplements daily.

After analyzing the pros and cons of gastric sleeve surgery, it's clear why doctors recommend this procedure over other bariatric surgeries. The disadvantages are few, and the advantages when compared to other methods make VSG the superior choice. However, many people are torn between gastric bypass and sleeve surgery since the bypass procedure has slightly more impressive weight loss results. But, before you make up your mind, let's compare the two.

Bypass vs. the Sleeve

These two procedures are very similar; although the methods differ, it's all about reducing the size of the stomach and decreasing the amount of food a person can consume. They're both effective tools to lose weight in the long-term and improve obesity-related conditions such as diabetes, high cholesterol, high blood pressure, etc.

The gastric sleeve is a less complicated surgery, taking between 40 and 70 minutes to complete, whereas bypass surgery can take up to three hours.

Furthermore, gastric bypass patients may experience short-term complications such as bowel obstruction, ulcers, and internal hernias. The chance of sleeve patients developing any of these is close to zero.

If dietary constraints are the deciding factor for you, the changes you'll have to make will be the same for bypass and sleeve surgery. The main difference will be how much you can eat. If you opt for the gastric sleeve surgery, your stomach pouch will be able to hold up to three ounces. On the other hand, the gastric bypass will leave you with a stomach the size of a golf ball, which equates to 1 ounce.

Any decision of what bariatric surgery method to select should be made alongside your doctor. They will consider things like your age, overall health, weight, and expectations when making a decision. For example, gastric bypass surgery will usually be selected for patients with a Body Mass Index over 45, and not VSG.

Common Misconceptions

Before we move on to life after bariatric surgery, I think it is important to dispel some common myths about weight-loss surgery.

- **It's the easy way out.** If you're expecting a magic bullet, you won't get one. Although surgery will make your weight-loss journey significantly more manageable, you will still need to put in a lot of hard work and dedication.
- **It doesn't work in the long run.** Many people believe that surgery isn't a long-term solution since most people regain weight. Research shows that, compared to people who lost weight naturally, bariatric patients lost more weight and maintained their results (Huang et al., 2016).
- **It isn't safe.** The surgery itself is safer than other standard surgical procedures, with the risk of death within the first 30 days following surgery as low as 0.13% (Sudan et al., 2014). The risk of death due to various comorbidities is also significantly reduced. For example, the diabetes mortality rate decreases by more than 90% after bariatric surgery.

Chapter 2 A New Way of Life

It doesn't matter what bariatric surgery method you end up choosing; it is a life-altering procedure. For it to be successful, you will need to approach life and your food choices differently. This may be more challenging than going through the actual surgery and recovery process. Here is how you will have to alter your outlook.

Before we get to your mindset, you will have to prepare those around you. You may even consider involving those closest to you in the process. This will make it easier to understand what exactly is happening and how they can best support you. Of course, you won't have to share your decision to have bariatric surgery with those who aren't part of your inner circle, or those who might only have negative things to say. Deciding to have surgery is personal, and I suggest you only discuss it with people you know will support and encourage you. If someone who you thought would be understanding turns out against it, don't let the comments dissuade you. It's usually because they are not understanding the process, or they are afraid of the unknown and what can happen.

Remind yourself that the only person you're held accountable for is yourself. Keep your head held high and surprise those who doubt you with a remarkable transformation!

Now, let's move on to you and your new way of life.

Eat Without Fear

You will have to learn how to eat again. After your surgery, you will first start consuming liquids and gradually move on to eat a balanced diet of almost all the foods you used to enjoy. In the beginning, you may feel a little overwhelmed with not knowing what is safe to eat, and this fear may lead to you to avoid eating altogether. This is never a good idea; if you starve yourself, the chances of binging on the wrong foods is more likely.

Recognize that asking for help is okay. You need to rely on medical professionals to share with you any information that will put your fears at ease. They will tell you precisely what you should and shouldn't eat, which should put your mind at ease. You may also consider joining a bariatric support group where you can share what you're going through and get advice from people who've been where you are or who are currently struggling with the same thing. Support is paramount, especially in the early days when you are still finding your feet.

You may be scared that your old eating habits will come back and before you know it, you'll undo the benefits of the weight-loss surgery. This is the moment the negative thinking needs to be silenced—tell yourself this time is different. I know many people who get bariatric surgery do so because they have spent their whole lives yo-yo dieting, which is their last attempt at success. Well, weight-loss surgery gives you a great head start, which will be a massive help.

It will be difficult (near impossible) for you to slip back to the "old you" if you change your mindset to one of victory. Always keep in your mind that this is not "just another diet," it is a permanent lifestyle change. Commit to yourself!

Be Compassionate

Probably the most important thing you can do is to be kind to yourself—everything else will flow from it. Your self-talk directly affects your happiness, and this will influence how easy it will be for you to stick to these changes in the long run. To practice self-compassion, you have to be kind, mindful, and accept that you're only human.

Accept that all patients who undergo weight-loss surgery will make mistakes. The triumph lies in how you react to any slip-ups. If you're sympathetic with yourself instead of cruel and criticizing, the chances of sliding back into old habits are far less. Remember that we're all human; embrace your victories but your defeats, too. Leave no space for self-denigration when you do fail. Consider that maybe your mind just needed a break from constantly focusing on your goals. If you're afraid of this happening again, do something relaxing. Meditation is a great way to quiet the mind and maintain perspective.

Whatever the reasons behind any blunders, don't fixate on them—move on and get excited about your future.

Learn New Eating Habits

It will be necessary for you to adjust the way you eat, especially just after surgery, as your body gets used to this change. But it goes further than that, and you will have to change your relationship with food entirely for long-term success. Some doctors may even suggest you see a therapist to help you understand why you were overweight in the first place. If you're like me, you eat when you're bored, stressed, or sad. The only thing I found that could snap me out of this behavior was to see someone who gave me the tools to overcome the unhealthy connection I had with food.

It's difficult—in society today, food plays such a central role—almost all celebrations are around food of some sort. This is why it is extra vital for you to take back your power and stop letting food take control. For example, if you're an emotional eater, learn healthy ways to cope with your feelings without using food as a distraction. If you always eat when you're lonely, why not call a friend if you'd like some company? Food is not your friend; it is fuel for your body.

There are various ways you can shift the emphasis from eating to some or other activity. Instead of meeting friends for dinner, why not plan a day to meet up and exercise or go hiking? If you give food less of a fundamental role in life, it will lose its grip.

Here are three tips to keep you on track.

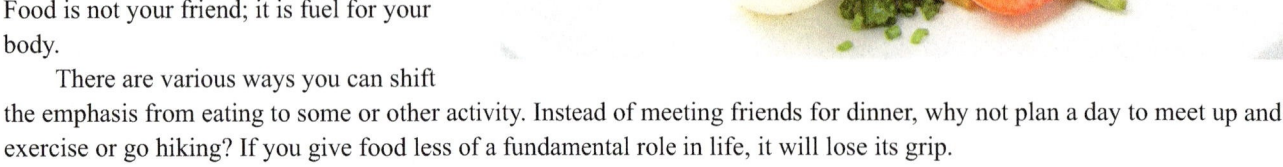

1. Stick to the Basics

Be mindful of the fact that it is going to take some time for you to understand the dos and don'ts of your new diet. The most crucial time is the first few weeks after surgery. You will have to stick to the rules to not get sick. It's not a matter of ifs or buts. After the initial transition period, you'll be able to eat normally. But always keep in mind that overeating is not what you should ever aim for—not only will you feel ill, you'll be working against your body and the weight-loss surgery. Keep the basics of the bariatric diet in mind, and that way, you'll know exactly what your stomach's limits are and what foods you can have.

2. Beat the Cravings

Regrettably, for many people who've struggled with weight throughout their life, giving in to cravings is like flipping an 'on' switch. Telling yourself that you'll eat only one Oreo usually turns into an entire sleeve or box. This binge-type behavior snowballs into disappointment and self-hate, which can lead to more binging. Instead of giving in immediately, stop, and check your motives. When you do decide it is worth giving in to your cravings, try to manage your actions. You don't want it to spiral and you end up overindulging the entire weekend.

3. Stop Eating When You're Full

Your body will tell you when it has had enough, and it is up to you to listen and resist taking another bite. If you practice mindful eating, it will be much easier to stop when you've had enough. I suggest you turn off the TV and remove any distractions that take your attention away from eating. A lot of the time, we're so focused on an episode of our favorite show that we forget we're eating—it's a mechanical action. Before you know it, you've eaten more than your body can take, and you're left feeling bloated and nauseous.

A huge part of your long-term success depends on your relationship with food. You must take away any control it has over you. Here are some tips to help you get started

- Find strategies that help you manage your emotions to stop emotional eating. Similarly, find ways to break the pattern of eating if you're in a bad mood.
- Go for a walk when you get a craving. They only last for 15 to 20 minutes, 30 at most, so if you can distract yourself for that span of time, you'll beat the urge to give in (Ledochowski et al., 2015).
- Always carry healthy snacks with you when you know you're going to have a busy day. This will prevent you from having to choose less healthy options when you get peckish.
- It's a good idea to make a shopping list before you go to the grocery store. If you stick to buying only what is on the list, you will avoid impulse buying unhealthy food that doesn't fit in with your gastric diet.

How to Eat

For the first few weeks after surgery, how you eat will be just as important as what you eat. Besides that, you will have to be conscious of the size of the bites you take when you start to eat normally again. Considering that your stomach is so much smaller, it can only tolerate a certain amount of food at a time, so you will have to take smaller bites, chew up to 30 times, and eat for 20 to 30 minutes.

It's also recommended that you don't drink anything while you eat. You don't want to fill your stomach with liquid instead of food. There's also a possibility that fluid will flush food out of your stomach too quickly.

Another issue you will face is forcing yourself to eat when you're not hungry. Since there is a massive reduction in the ghrelin—the hormone that promotes hunger—you won't have an appetite. But you must meet your protein and nutrient needs. I suggest setting alarms throughout the day to remind you to eat when you're not hungry. Since your stomach is so small, you may need to eat up to six times a day to get all the nutrients you need.

To prepare yourself for all these changes, you can start learning these new habits even before surgery. You can also follow the recipes in this cookbook so long to get used to eating a bariatric diet.

Here are some small ways you can start to form sleeve-friendly eating habits.

1. Downsize your plates and bowls.
2. Teach yourself to take smaller bites.
3. Chew your food at least 25 times before swallowing.
4. Don't inhale your food. Eat slowly.
5. Stop eating when you're full. A sigh, burp, hiccup, and even a runny nose may signal that your body has had enough.

Chapter 3 Your Diet After Bariatric Surgery

I'm going to guess that you are very familiar with various weight-loss diets. You've probably tried all of them but failed to stick to it for whatever reason. The decision to have VSG isn't made overnight and usually comes after years of trying and failing to lose weight. So, you most likely are familiar with the way diets work and the nutritional benefits of specific foods. This counts to your advantage while adapting to a bariatric diet.

VSG Nutrition

You don't need to be a dietician or a nutrition expert to understand the eating plan I will share in this cookbook. There are some basic principles you need to keep in mind, and that's it! The recipes you'll find in this book take each of these considerations into account for your convenience. But let's first look at how the macronutrients (protein, fat, carbohydrates) will need to be adapted to the bariatric diet.

Protein

Protein is the most important macronutrient following surgery. Protein gives you energy and will preserve your muscles as you lose weight. It also takes longer to break down than carbohydrates, so that you will feel satiated for longer. It is also less calorie-dense than fat, which means, out of all the macronutrients, protein is the best post-op. The first two weeks after surgery, you won't be eating protein solids but will instead drink protein-rich smoothies. Later on, there will be a bigger mix of meals. This makes this cookbook invaluable as it will give you a variety of ideas while keeping your protein needs in mind.

Eating enough protein will also make your body heal from surgery faster. It is recommended that you consume between 2.11 to 3.52 ounces of protein a day based on ideal body weight. Counting how much protein you eat is the only way to make sure all your needs are being met. You can use an online food tracking app if you like to do things electronically. If you're old-school and prefer doing it by hand, here's a handy table of protein-rich foods, the recommended portion sizes, and the protein per ounce.

Protein Sources	Portion Size	Protein (ounces)*
Beek, pork, poultry, fish	2 ounces	0.49
Scallops, shrimp	3 ounces	0.63
Turkey, ham, roast beef, chicken, or other lunch meat	2 ounces	0.35
Eggs	1 large	0.24
Egg whites	2 large	0.28
Fat-free, 1% or 2% cottage or ricotta cheese	½ cup	0.49
Cheddar, mozzarella, Swiss, and other natural cheese	1 ounce	0.24
Non-fat Greek yogurt	6 ounces (3/4 cup)	0.52
Lentils (cooked)	½ cup	0.31
Beans (cooked)	½ cup	0.31
Avoid: High-fat foods such as cream, whole milk, fatty cuts of beef or pork, and skin on poultry.		

***Always check the label on foods as protein content may vary.**

If you find it difficult to reach sufficient protein levels, you can use protein shakes, powders, or bars.

Carbohydrates

Although protein should be your main focus, carbohydrates are a quick energy source and are vital in various metabolic functions. The first few weeks after surgery, you will eat little to no carbs. Your body will instead metabolize fat stores and use

Chapter 3: Your Diet After Bariatric Surgery | 11

the protein you eat as a fuel source.

When you do reintroduce carbohydrates into your diet, remember that not all carbs are created equal. You get simple and complex carbs. The simple type is digested faster than complex carbs, which leads to a blood sugar spike that isn't good for your overall health and weight loss goals. Foods containing white refined flour, a lot of sugar, and are highly processed are considered simple carbs.

On the bariatric diet, you will consume only complex carbohydrates such as whole-grain foods, fruits, and veggies. These foods are rich in fiber, vitamins, and minerals and break down slower, preventing unnecessary fluctuating blood sugar levels.

Once you're allowed to eat normally, you should aim to eat 35 to 45 percent of your daily calories in carbohydrates.

Carbohydrate Sources	Portion Size	Carbohydrate (ounces)
Fresh fruit	1 serving = ½ cup Recommended: 2 to 3 servings per day after initial liquid and soft food diet.	1.58
Vegetables	1 serving = 1 cup Recommended: 4 servings per day after initial liquid and soft food diet.	0.52
Oatmeal	½ cup	0.49
Whole-grain bread	1 slice	0.52
Brown or white rice	½ cup	0.81
Whole-wheat pasta	1/3 cup	0.98
Barley	1/3 cup	0.81
Ancient grains (quinoa, millet, spelt, farrow)	1/3 cup	0.52
Avoid: Refined grains, cookies, cakes, pastries, candies, fruit juice, and soda.		

Fats

You will have to keep an eye on your fat intake since it is such a calorie-dense food—overeat fat, and you'll stall your weight loss. That doesn't mean you shouldn't eat it at all. We need dietary fat to help absorb fat-soluble vitamins like A, D, E, and K.

There are two types of fat; saturated and unsaturated. Saturated fat should be limited as it can increase your cholesterol and chances of a heart attack. Processed foods, coconut oil, full-fat dairy, butter, beef, pork, and chicken contain saturated fat.

Unsaturated fat comes from nuts, seeds, and olives. Fish is also a good source of these healthy fats. To lower your cholesterol levels and reduce your risk of heart disease, unsaturated fat is your friend.

Keep an eye on food labels of processed foods. These products may claim to be fat-free or low fat but usually contain hidden sugar or sodium to put some flavor back. Always choose low-fat or non-fat when it comes to dairy products, but opt for full-fat foods in the form of nuts, seeds, avocadoes, olives, and fatty fish.

In the beginning, you will consume minimal amounts of fat. However, in the long-term, you're looking at 30 percent of your daily calories from fats—less than 7 percent of this should be from saturated fats.

Fat Sources	Portion Sizes (one serving)	Fat (ounces)
Avocado	1 tablespoon	0.49
Chia	2 teaspoons	0.63
Olive oil	1 teaspoon	0.15
Almonds	6 tablespoons	0.12
Walnuts	2 tablespoons	0.18
Peanuts	10 tablespoons	0.17
Nut butters	2 teaspoons	0.17

Limit: Butter, palm and coconut oil, and full-fat dairy.
Avoid: Animal fats, fried foods, margarine containing trans fats, and food high in saturated fats.

Vitamins and Supplements

You will need to take a vitamin and mineral supplement for the rest of your life. If you're lucky, any deficiencies you have due to your gastric sleeve may disappear once you reach your goal weight, but it's best to err on the side of caution. You should follow up with your bariatric medical team on a regular basis to test your nutrients but never decide on your own to stop your supplementation.

Some of the most common deficiencies include:

Vitamin D: The recommended daily dosage is 3.000 IU, but it can be more, depending on the levels already in your blood.

Calcium: This is important for bone health—drink between 1.200 and 1.500 mg per day, divided into two or three doses.

Iron: Although it is not standard to recommend iron after weight-loss surgery, your doctor may do so your base-line levels are low.

Vitamin B12: Your doctor will routinely check your B12 levels. This vitamin is vital for normal nerve function and is regrettably usually impaired after VSG. You can either drink it as a daily supplement of 1.00 mcg per day or ask for an injection.

Some tips on drinking your supplements:

1. Drink your vitamins close to mealtime. A lot of vitamins are best absorbed with food.

2. Don't use gummy vitamins. They usually contain a lot of sugar, which means they're high in calories. Furthermore, most brands don't provide the 100 to 200 percent recommended daily allowance. If you prefer a chewable over liquid or pills, discuss it with your doctor and ask for a recommendation.

3. Look for the USP verified symbol. There are a lot of herbal supplements out there claiming to contain everything you need. Since the FDA doesn't regulate herbal medicines, there's no way for you to know if the claims they make are valid. Instead, look for USP-verified vitamins and minerals; that way, you know that you're getting high-quality products. You may also consider buying vitamins targeted for bariatric surgery patients. These supplements are usually more expensive, but they take the guesswork out of post-of bariatric supplementation.

Stay Hydrated

This will be your main focus after surgery, considering that dehydration is the most common complication (Ivanics, 2019). It will be challenging at first—a lot of us are used to enjoying a glass of water with our food, something you're not allowed to do after bariatric surgery. You won't be able to drink a large amount of fluid at once but will have to get into the habit of drinking small sips throughout the day.

I also suggest you take a more proactive approach and carry a water bottle with you. This way, you won't get stuck somewhere without access to water. You'll also be more conscious of how much you're drinking if you have a bottle in your hand where you can see the fluid getting less.

Fluid Sources: Water/Milk/Soy milk/Protein shakes/Decaffeinated coffee or tea/Non-carbonated, sugar-free drinks

It is recommended that you drink at least 64 ounces (eight cups) of fluids per day. You won't be able to meet this target straight after surgery, but this should be an achievable goal in the long-term.

Tips to help you stay hydrated:
- Drink a glass of water after waking up in the morning before you eat or drink anything else.
- Sip on a liquid between each small meal.
- Always carry a water bottle with you; stainless steel reusable is best!
- If you find that you forget to drink, set alarms to remind you.

What about alcohol?

After VSG, your stomach's ability to process alcohol will be severely hindered. There is an enzyme in your stomach responsible for breaking down alcohol, and since most of your stomach has been removed, there is not enough meaning even a small amount will leave you intoxicated. Moreover, considering that your body mass is smaller than it was and the fact that you're only capable of ingesting small amounts of food, this will amplify the intoxication.

The fact that your blood-alcohol level will peak so much faster means the dehydration that follows drinking alcohol will also happen sooner than you expect.

With that being said, the answer to if you may drink alcohol after bariatric isn't exactly a n 'no.' You can indulge within moderation while keeping the above factors in mind. Ideally, you should wait three to 12 months after surgery before you drink anything alcoholic.

One last word of warning: transference addiction is a reality (Obesity Action Coalition, 2016). Patients who have a history of addiction may end up replacing their food addiction with other addictive behaviors, such as overconsumption of alcohol. If you notice any worrying changes in behavior, including excessive gambling, shopping, or other addictive behaviors, discuss it with your bariatric health team.

Some tips for drinking alcohol safely after bariatric surgery:
- Do not drink and eat at the same time.
- Consume low-calorie options and alcohol without added sugar. Whiskey on the rocks or red wine are good options.
- Avoid anything carbonated.
- Drink extra water when you are consuming alcohol.
- Eat a snack before you start drinking.

Keep Things Naturally Sweet

If you're used to eating the standard American diet, you'll know that your threshold for sweetness is higher than it was a few years ago. Everything is getting sugary and sweeter, making it more difficult to "kick the habit." The reality is that sugar is a drug, and we're always looking for our next fix (Avena et al., 2008).

VSG allows you to beat your sugar addiction. With this reset, you'll be able to jump start new eating habits. I'm not saying it will be easy, especially keeping in mind the pleasure centers in our brain that light up when we eat sugar. But, it is possible to retrain yourself to appreciate natural sweetness. Natural is full of candy; we just have to make the right decisions. Instead of reaching for a sugary dessert, you can eat some fresh berries. If your chocolate craving becomes overwhelming, add some 100 percent cocoa powder to a protein shake, and you have a delicious chocolate milkshake! The options are endless, and it's up to you to make the right choices.

When it comes to eating fruit, they contain many good, naturally occurring sugars your body likes. This is often forgotten since most sugars are lumped into one big category, so good sugars end up labeled as bad. The fact is that whole fruits have no added sugars. The phytochemicals and fiber content in fruit also delay the absorption of these natural sugars, meaning you won't experience any nasty blood sugar spikes as you would with refined sugar.

Just a few things to consider when it comes to eating fruit:
- Since protein is the most important macronutrient, eat it first, then fruits and vegetables, and other types of food.
- Fruit is high in calories, and carbohydrates, so don't overeat it, or you'll slow down your weight loss progress.

Foods to Avoid

Although the long-term goal is living as normal a life as possible, you will have to be mindful of what you put in your body. When you read up on VSG, you will see a lot of patients mention dumping syndrome. This is what happens when you eat foods you were supposed to avoid post-op. It's nothing to be scared of as it is entirely preventable. During the first three months after your VSG, there are foods you have to avoid. As time passes, you can slowly start reintroducing some of these foods into your diet, except for high-sugar and fried foods. These foods are known for causing dumping syndrome in not only bypass patients but also sleeve patients.

There are two types of dumping syndrome; early and late.

Early dumping syndrome will happen a short while after eating specific foods and is caused by the rapid emptying of the stomach. Symptoms include sweating, a rapid pulse, lightheadedness, a desire to lie down, nausea, and diarrhea. It is more common than late dumping and will pass as soon as the food has made its way out of your system.

Late dumping syndrome will only occur one to three hours after eating. You may feel shaky, dizzy, break out in cold sweats, experience confusion and anxiety, and feel hungry again. This is caused by hormonal changes caused by specific food and will pass when the food is out of your system.

Liquids	Proteins	Carbs	Fats	Other
Carbonated drinks	Breaded and deep-fried protein	Rice	Raw nuts and seeds	Asparagus stalks
Alcohol	Dry and tough meat	Pasta	Fried foods	Raw celery
Caffeine		Bread	Greasy foods	Coconut
Fruit juice		Dried fruits	Nut butter	Sweetened sauces or condiments
Sugary beverages		Skin of fruit		Cookies
		Fresh pineapple		Candy
		Popcorn		
		Granola and bran cereal		

Plan Your Meals

What is that saying again? "Failing to plan is planning to fail." This is very true when it comes to the long-term success of your VSG. Meal planning should form an integral part of your new lifestyle. If you take the time to map out your meals for the coming week—I don't mean down to every ingredient—you'll know if you have all the ingredients you need to prepare your meals.

It is particularly important in the days following surgery since you will have to keep an eye on your protein intake. By planning it all out, you can build your meals around protein and add fruit, vegetables, and grains.

Meal prep isn't limited to listing what you'll eat but includes pre-batching these meals. I am a big supporter of cooking meals for the week because you'll know there is a healthy meal waiting for you when you get home—removing any temptation of buying something unhealthy.

In essence, you'll be creating your own "frozen dinners," and you'll know exactly what's in them and that they're made according to the bariatric diet. In this cookbook, I include a lot of meals you can safely pre-cook, reheat, and eat.

Stock Your Kitchen

To cook mouth-watering sleeve-friendly meals, you need to stock up on some essentials—not just food but also some nifty must-have gadgets.

Food

You now know that the bariatric diet consists of protein, high-fiber carbs, and healthy fats, and can build your food stock around that. Make sure you have tons of different meats, fish and seafood, eggs, low-fat dairy, and legumes in your kitchen. You will also need some non-starchy vegetables, whole fruits, nuts and seeds, and various whole grains.

Here's a mini shopping list for when you first set up your bariatric kitchen.

- Almond flour
- Dried lentils
- Canned beans
- Dried spices and herbs
- Canned tuna, chicken, and salmon
- Eggs
- Olive oil
- Nuts and seeds
- Unsweetened pasta sauce
- Oats
- Whole wheat flour
- Low-sodium broth (vegetable, beef, and chicken)
- Frozen fruit
- Frozen vegetables
- Frozen meats
- Low- or no-fat dairy

If you still have food in your cupboard from your pre-VSG life, I suggest you donate anything that you can't use to a local food bank or a family in need.

Do a sweep of your kitchen, and if you see any of the following, clear it out.

- Boxed potatoes
- Bread
- Baked beans
- Cookies
- Chips
- Candy
- Cereal
- Crackers
- Frozen desserts
- Dried fruit
- High-carb frozen meals
- Sugary condiments
- High-fat products
- Refined pasta
- White rice
- Popcorn
- Caffeine

Gadgets

Who doesn't like a kitchen gadget that can make your life easier? You won't need fancy tools to prepare any of the meals in this cookbook—basic equipment such as knives, measuring cups, pots, and pans. There are a few tools I suggest you add to your kitchen to make cooking more comfortable and less time-consuming.

Mixer: It doesn't just mix, it whisks and can knead the dough.

Spiralizer and vegetable peeler: A very handy tool if you plan on making pasta dupes such as zucchini noodles. A peeler is essential as you will have to remove the skins from fruits and vegetables in the first few months after your surgery.

Immersion blender: Puree soup and sauces or other dishes while the pot or pan is still on the stove.

Muffin tin: You can use this to help with portion control.

Slow cooker: A great way to save time cooking.

Air fryer: Considering that you're not allowed to eat deep-fried food on the bariatric diet, air-fried food is the next best thing. You eat less than a teaspoon oil, and your food will come out nice and crispy.

Your First 8 Weeks After Surgery

After sleeve surgery, your body will need time to get used to the new stomach. To help it along, your post-op diet will be divided into various textures starting with liquids, moving on to purées, then soft food, and eventually eating regular textured foods. Your doctor will determine how long you will stay in each phase, but I will share the general guidelines.

Week 1 and 2

These two weeks are all about getting and staying hydrated. As mentioned earlier, dehydration is the first complication post-op and can leave you feeling ill reasonably quickly. Weeks one and two will set the foundation and get you into the habit of drinking enough fluids daily—long after these two weeks have passed.

Here are some factors you will have to keep in mind during this time:
- Water comes first. Other clear liquids and any protein-rich shakes can be consumed after water. Try to drink at least 64 ounces of water a day.
- Shakes and smoothies shouldn't contain any seeds or pulp.
- Drink high-protein milk between meals to increase your protein consumption.

Week 3

You will now be able to introduce soft, puréed food to your diet. Your body has done a lot of healing in the past two weeks, and the high protein-intake has helped significantly. Now it is more capable of absorbing nutrients and is reverting to proper digestion. The focus during the next week should be on portion size; you're not used to how much food your stomach can handle, so you will have to be careful. It's best to limit portions to 2 to 3 ounces during this time.

You can purée soft meats, fruits, cooked veggies, eggs, legumes, low-fat dairy, low-fat soups, and low-fiber cooked cereal. Just keep in mind that there should be no solid pieces in it at all—aim for a smooth paste. Also, don't neglect your hydration. You still have to drink water, as well as protein shakes during week three.

Some tips to get through this week:
- If you experience any discomfort while eating, make sure you're not eating too fast or taking bites that are too large.
- If you're not hungry, continue to drink your protein shakes. You must keep meeting your daily protein goals.
- Don't neglect your hydration. Remember, fluids first, then protein, and lastly, other foods.
- Try to eat ½ a cup of food for each meal.
- Continue to drink high-protein milk between each meal to up your protein intake.
- You can use water, milk, broth, or yogurt to thin foods to your desired consistency.

Week 4, 5, and 6

Your body is used to digesting puréed food now and is ready for food with more substance. As you introduce different types of softer protein into your diet, you can start to drink fewer protein shakes, but only if you're eating enough protein otherwise.

For food to be classified as 'soft,' it has to be tender enough for you to easily cut through it with a fork. Don't overwhelm your body by eating various types of soft foods in one meal—stick to adding one or two types of food at a time. Lean ground beef or poultry, soft and flaky fish, eggs, cottage cheese, soft cheese, yogurt, cooked vegetables, and canned fruits are good options to include on your menu in weeks six and seven.

Portions will vary, but you can aim for ½ cup of food per meal. Always adjust the nutritional information based on what you consumed to make sure you don't miss your protein target of 2.11 and 2.82 ounces per day. Again, don't forget to stay hydrated!

Some helpful tips for weeks four, five, and six:
- If you are experiencing discomfort after adding soft food, try eating something with more moisture.
- Set alarms to remind you to eat if you discover that you lack an appetite.
- Only introduce one or two new foods at a time.

Weeks 7 and 8

Congratulations! You made it. You have completed the transition diet and can now add a variety of textures back into your diet. This doesn't mean you should forget to focus on portion size and making sure you're eating enough protein! These two aspects will continue with you throughout your life. Also, stay away from high-fat and high-carb foods.

As weeks four, five, and six, only introduced one or two new foods at a time, be mindful that some foods may cause some discomfort.

Portions will vary, but you should be able to comfortably ingest ½ to one cup of food each meal. Continue to reach your target of 48 ounces of fluids and 2.11 ounces of protein daily.

Going forward, remember to:
- Eat three meals with two snacks a day.
- Drink high-protein milk between meals to meet your protein target until you are able to eat enough protein.
- If you feel ill after introducing more solids, go back to following the soft food diet of weeks six and seven.
- Don't forget to drink water to keep yourself hydrated.

Dealing with Social Occasions

Humans like to gather around a table, enjoy some good food and a glass of wine. There's nothing wrong with your innate need to be social, but for someone who underwent weight-loss surgery, it can be a source of anxiety. There are certain limitations you have to consider when going out, but you should let it hold you back.

Dining Out

With some planning and quick thinking, you can join your friends at any restaurant and order with ease.
- Check the menu ahead of time. You can check the website, or if you know where the restaurant is, head in for a quick coffee and look over what you can order beforehand.
- There's no rule stopping you from ordering an appetizer or side-dish as an entrée.
- Do not be adventurous when eating out. Choose foods you know work well with your stomach.
- Remember the basics: no deep-fried foods, carbs, high-fat food, sweet carbonated drinks, or desserts.
- Divide your plate into two. You can eat the leftovers the next day.

During the Holidays

Holidays are full of temptation—food and alcohol at every turn. This combined with the excitement of spending time with family and friends may be enough to cause some missteps. Here are some tips on how to deal with parties and celebrations after you've had bariatric surgery.
- Eat a meal or snack that is high in protein before the party.
- Don't sit close to any appetizers or the buffet tables. You don't want to fall into the "it's there, so let me take one bite" trap.

- If you're asked to bring a side dish, make one that you'll be able to eat.
- Always choose a small portion of protein and vegetables from the menu or at a buffet.
- If you don't want to drink alcohol, but you're afraid everyone will make a fuss, fill a cocktail glass with water, and add some juice and a lemon wedge. Voilà! A sleeve-friendly mocktail.

FAQs

Vertical gastric sleeve surgery is such a life-changing surgery. I'm sure you have even more questions whirling around in your head than the ones I answered in this cookbook. Don't worry. I have a good idea of what you may want to know based on the questions I asked when I first learned about VGS and bariatric surgery in general.

1. Can doctors refuse to do a VSG on me?

It's not so much that they'll refuse but recommend you get gastric bypass surgery instead in some instances. If you have difficulty swallowing (esophageal dysmotility) or if your food stays in your stomach too long (gastroparesis), gastric bypass is the better option. The same applies if you have severe GERD.

2. Do I need to change my diet before getting surgery?

Technically, you don't need to change your eating habits before VSG, but I suggest you try. If you start to make healthy changes to what you eat and create positive eating patterns beforehand, you'll have an easier time adjusting to the bariatric diet post-op. It is overwhelming to implement all the changes at once—counting protein, drinking more water, giving up fast food, remembering your multivitamin daily, all while recovering from surgery. Establishing some of these habits weeks or months before the operation will make the adjustment process so much more comfortable.

However, your doctor may place you on a pre-operative program to help you lose weight before surgery. This is to decrease belly fat and reduce the liver size, which will make the operation safer for you.

3. How is it possible to pull such a large part of the stomach through such a small incision?

The stomach can stretch significantly—holding up to 128 ounces of food when fully expanded. During the VSG, a tube will remove all the gas and liquids from the stomach. This decompresses the stomach, making it possible to remove up to 80%. The fact that the incision is 1.11 inches at most means you will experience a lot less pain after surgery.

4. Will I keep the weight off after surgery?

The short answer is yes; research shows sustained weight loss after VSG. However, as I mentioned earlier in the book, bariatric surgery is not magic—you will need to do your part to ensure and maintain success.

5. Can VSG cause heartburn?

The jury is out on this one as some patients report increased Gastroesophageal Reflux Disease (GERD), while others describe a decrease. It seems if the surgeon does not remove the upper part of the stomach (fundus), GERD is more prevalent in patients. This is something you can discuss with your doctor to determine if they pay extra attention to removing the fundus.

But don't worry, if you happen to be one of the people who get GERD as a side-effect, it can easily be managed with antacid medication and diet changes.

6. I haven't met my protein goal for the day. What can I eat to boost my protein intake?

Don't worry too much if you don't always hit your protein targets—if you eat enough protein 80 percent of the time, you'll be fine. To up your protein for the day, choose something that doesn't take a lot of time to prepare. Low-fat cottage cheese, Greek yogurt, eggs, and lunch meat are good options, but you can also drink a protein shake if you're not in the mood to eat anything. You can eat a high-protein breakfast the next day to make up for the shortfall you had the day before.

7. What protein powders are the best?

I think the protein and supplement aisle is probably the most overwhelming section of any grocery store. There are so many products—each claiming to be better than the other. I suggest going for whey protein isolate. Not only is it easy for the body to absorb, but it also contains high amounts of essential amino acids. If you're looking for a vegetarian or vegan option, you can try soy protein isolate. It's best to go for the unflavored kind since they are low in calories and free from artificial ingredients. If you have no other option than choosing a flavored protein powder, always select the sugar-free kind.

8. I am always so full after eating my protein that there's no room for vegetables and fruits. This can't be healthy?

I know that eating only protein for weeks may not seem like the healthiest thing to do, but keep in mind that it is only temporary. While your body is getting used to a smaller stomach and the subsequent digestion changes, you will drink a multivitamin that will make up for any nutrients you'll miss out on during this time. As you move from liquids to purée, and finally to regular eating patterns, your stomach will adjust, and you will have space for food other than protein.

9. There is so much conflicting information about carbohydrates. Am I allowed to eat carbs after VSG?

Your stomach will struggle to digest carbs for a few months after your surgery. This is why it is best to limit your carb intake. Another reason why most doctors suggest you cut carbs out of your diet is to help you lose weight. Carbohydrates are high in calories and will cause your weight loss to stall if eaten in excess. It also doesn't contain nearly the amount of vitamins and minerals fruits and veggies do. Considering that your stomach can only take so much, it is best to prioritize foods that will meet your nutritional needs.

10. How do I keep on track if I don't have support from my spouse?

It is difficult when the people in your household continue to eat junk food while you have to stick to the bariatric diet. The first thing you can do is communicate with your loved ones and let them know what you need. If they're not sure what your goals are and how you plan to reach them, you can't expect them to be considerate. However, here are some tips you can try when your family isn't willing to make a lifestyle change with you.

- Ask your family only to keep treats in the house that you can resist.
- Take up an activity that will keep your mind occupied or distract you when the Oreos in the cupboard is calling your name. Go for a walk, read, or call a support buddy—do anything you can to find an outlet that isn't eating.
- Keep healthy snacks or quick meals on hand for you and your family. If there is food in the house, you minimize the chances of a family member getting take-out because they're too hungry or tired to cook.

Lastly, if you're unlucky and your family doesn't care about your health journey, put all the unhealthy food in a cupboard with a lock and give only them keys. You'll still have to watch them eat these foods, but at least you won't have direct access to it when a craving strike.

Chapter 4 Full Liquid Foods

1. Chamomile Blossom Tea   22
2. Rose Hip Tea   22
3. Ginger Tea   22
4. Southwest-Style Chicken Bone Broth   22
5. Refreshing Mint Lemonade   23
6. Cool-as-a-Cucumber Water   23
7. Christmas Punch   23
8. Mulled Blueberry Warmer   23
9. High-Protein Milk   24
10. Spiced Milk   24
11. Protein Mochaccino   24
12. Savory Beef Bone Broth   24
13. Hot Chocolate   25
14. Berry Blast Protein Shake   25
15. Vanilla Apple Pie Protein Shake   25
16. Black-and-White Peanut Butter Shake   25
17. Banana-Chocolate Shake   26
18. Chicken Broth   26
19. Tomato Soup   26

Chamomile Blossom Tea

Prep time: 10 minutes | Cook time: 5 minutes | Serves 1

1 cup water

1 tablespoon fragrant dried chamomile blossoms, crushed

1. In a small saucepan, heat water to a boil. 2. Remove pan from heat, add chamomile blossoms to water and stir to combine. Cover pan and let steep for about 10 minutes. 3. Strain tea through a metal mesh strainer and serve immediately. Enjoy!

Per Serving

calories: 2 | fat: 0g | protein: 0g | carbs: 0g | fiber: 0g | sugar: 0g | sodium: 7mg

Rose Hip Tea

Prep time: 1 minute | Cook time: 5 minutes | Serves 1

1 tablespoon whole dried rose hips, lightly crushed

1 cup water

1. In a small saucepan, mix rose hips into water, cover pan and heat to a boil. Reduce heat and simmer for about 5 minutes. 2. Strain rose hip tea through a metal mesh strainer and serve immediately. Enjoy!

Per Serving

calories: 13 | fat: 0g | protein: 0g | carbs: 3g | fiber: 2g | sugar: 0g | sodium: 5mg

Ginger Tea

Prep time: 15 minutes | Cook time: 15 minutes | Serves 1

1 piece fresh ginger root (about ½ inch)

1 cup water

1. In a small saucepan, heat water to a boil. 2. Peel ginger root and cut into thin slices. 3. Add ginger root to water. Remove pan from heat, cover and let tea steep for about 10 minutes. 4. Remove ginger from tea, sweeten if desired and serve immediately. Enjoy!

Per Serving

calories: 2 | fat: 0g | protein: 0g | carbs: 0g | fiber: 0g | sugar: 0g | sodium: 0mg

Southwest-Style Chicken Bone Broth

Prep time: 5 minutes | Cook time: 5 to 8 hours | Makes 8 cups

Nonstick cooking spray
4 large carrots, peeled and chopped
1 medium red onion, quartered
1 large tomato, quartered
1 red bell pepper, sliced
1 (5- to 7-pound / 2.3- to 3.2-kg) whole chicken
12 to 16 cups water
1 teaspoon salt
1 teaspoon ground cumin
1 teaspoon dried cilantro
2 bay leaves

1. Preheat the oven to 400ºF (205ºC). Coat a shallow broiler pan with nonstick cooking spray. 2. Arrange the carrot, onion, tomato, and bell pepper in an even layer in the pan. Place the chicken in the pan and roast for 90 minutes or more (about 20 minutes per pound of chicken), until a thermometer inserted in the thigh reads 165ºF (74ºC) and the juices run clear. 3. Remove the pan from the oven and remove the meat from carcass, setting aside for other recipes. 4. Place the carcass and vegetables in a large pot. Add enough water to the pot to cover the carcass and vegetables completely. Add the salt, cumin, cilantro, and bay leaves to the pot and bring to a rolling boil. 5. Reduce the heat to medium and simmer for at least 4 hours, or longer for increased flavor. Supervise the pot during the simmering process, stirring a few times an hour. 6. Use a strainer spoon to remove the bones, meat, and vegetables from the pot. Enjoy the broth warm. 7. Store the leftover bone broth in an airtight container for up to 3 days or freeze for up to 1 year.

Per Serving (2 cups)

calories: 138 | fat: 2g | protein: 15g | carbs: 1g | fiber: 0g | sugar: 0g | sodium: 400mg

Refreshing Mint Lemonade

Prep time: 10 minutes | Cook time: 0 minutes | Makes 4 cups

Juice of 2 lemons
2 fresh mint sprigs

½ teaspoon stevia powder
4 cups water
Ice

1. In a small pitcher, use a wooden spoon or muddler to muddle together the lemon juice, mint leaves, and stevia to help bring out the oils in the mint. 2. Fill the pitcher with the water and ice, and serve.

Per Serving (1 cup)
calories: 5 | fat: 0g | protein: 0g | carbs: 1g | fiber: 0g | sugar: 0g | sodium: 0mg

Cool-as-a-Cucumber Water

Prep time: 5 minutes | Cook time: 0 minutes | Makes 8 cups

8 cups water
1 lemon, sliced

1 lime, sliced
½ cucumber, sliced
2 fresh mint sprigs

1. In a 2¼-quart pitcher, combine the water, lemon, lime, cucumber, and mint. Muddle, if desired. 2. Chill for 30 minutes before drinking, or for best flavor, overnight.

Per Serving
calories: 8 | fat: 0g | protein: 0g | carbs: 3g | fiber: 1g | sugar: 0g | sodium: 1mg

Christmas Punch

Prep time: 5 minutes | Cook time: 0 minutes | Serves 4

2 rooibos tea bags
1 teaspoon granulated sweetener
6 whole cloves

1 cinnamon stick
1¼ cups light pomegranate and blueberry juice
Sliced plums and lemon wedges, to decorate (optional)

1. Put the tea bags, sweetener, cloves, and cinnamon stick into a large heatproof jug and pour over 2½ cups boiling water. Let stand for 5 minutes, then strain into a serving jug. 2. Add the pomegranate juice and stir well to mix. 3. Serve in glasses decorated with plum slices and lemon wedges, if desired.

Per Serving
calories: 9 | fat: 0g | protein: 0g | carbs: 2g | fiber: 0g | sugar: 1g | sodium: 12mg

Mulled Blueberry Warmer

Prep time: 5 minutes | Cook time: 0 minutes | Serves 4

1¼ pint no-added-sugar blueberry juice drink
1 teaspoon honey
4 ounces (113 g) mixed fresh or frozen berries
¼ teaspoon ground cinnamon

Small piece peeled fresh ginger, sliced
1 star anise
2 cloves
2 cinnamon sticks

1. Place the blueberry drink, honey, berries, and cinnamon in a blender and blend until smooth. 2. Pour the mixture into a pan and add the ginger, star anise, cloves, and cinnamon sticks. 3. Warm through gently without boiling. Strain and serve warm.

Per Serving
calories: 68 | fat: 0g | protein: 1g | carbs: 14g | fiber: 2g | sugar: 11g | sodium: 102mg

High-Protein Milk

Prep time: 5 minutes | Cook time: 0 minutes | Serves 4

4 cups low-fat milk

1⅓ cups instant nonfat dry milk powder

1. In a large pitcher, mix the milk and milk powder well. 2. Chill in the refrigerator for up to 5 days.

Per Serving

calories: 127 | fat: 3g | protein: 11g | carbs: 15g | fiber: 0g | sugar: 13g | sodium: 162mg

Spiced Milk

Prep time: 5 minutes | Cook time: 15 minutes | Serves 6

6 cups skim milk

4 cinnamon sticks

1. Heat milk to a simmer in a medium saucepan over medium heat. 2. Add cinnamon sticks to milk, reduce heat, cover pan and simmer gently for about 10 minutes. 3. Remove pan from heat and remove and discard cinnamon sticks. Serve milk immediately, or let cool and refrigerate to serve, or save for use in your favorite recipe. Enjoy!

Per Serving

calories: 89 | fat: 0g | protein: 8g | carbs: 13g | fiber: 1g | sugar: 12g | sodium: 129mg

Protein Mochaccino

Prep time: 5 minutes | Cook time: 0 minutes | Serves 1

½ cup cold skim milk
½ cup brewed strong decaffeinated coffee, chilled

1 serving (about 2 tablespoons) chocolate-flavored low-carb whey or soy protein isolate powder

1. Pour milk and coffee into a blender container, add protein powder and pulse until smooth. Serve immediately and enjoy!

Per Serving

calories: 165 | fat: 1g | protein: 33g | carbs: 9g | fiber: 2g | sugar: 6g | sodium: 428mg

Savory Beef Bone Broth

Prep time: 5 minutes | Cook time: 5 to 8 hours | Makes 8 cups

Nonstick cooking spray
1 medium yellow onion, chopped
1 cup diced celery
1 cup peeled, diced carrot
3 pounds (1.4 kg) beef bones

1 pound (454 g) stew beef
12 cups water
1 teaspoon salt
2 bay leaves
1 tablespoon minced garlic

1. Preheat the oven to 400ºF (205ºC). Coat a shallow roasting pan with cooking spray and set aside. 2. Arrange the onion, celery, and carrot in an even layer in the roasting pan. Place the beef bones and stew beef in the pan on top of the vegetables. Roast the bones, meat, and vegetables for 40 minutes, flipping the meat and bones halfway through the cooking time. 3. Remove the pan from the oven and place the bones, meat, and vegetables into a large stock pot. Add the water, salt, bay leaves, and garlic and bring to a rolling boil. 4. Reduce the heat to medium low and simmer for at least 4 hours. Supervise the pot during the simmering process, stirring a few times an hour. 5. Using a strainer spoon, remove the bones, meat, and vegetables from the pot. Enjoy the broth warm. 6. Store the leftover bone broth in an airtight container in the refrigerator for up to 3 days or freeze for up to 1 year.

Per Serving (2 cups)

calories: 138 | fat: 8g | protein: 13g | carbs: 2g | fiber: 1g | sugar: 0g | sodium: 465mg

Hot Chocolate

Prep time: 2 minutes | Cook time: 1 minute | Serves 1

1 tablespoon unsweetened cocoa powder
1 packet artificial sweetener (Splenda or Truvia)

1 cup skim milk

1. Mix cocoa and sweetener in a cup or mug. 2. Add ¼ cup milk and stir to make a paste. 3. Heat remaining ¾ cup milk in microwave on high for 45 seconds to 1 minute, or until hot. Add hot milk to cocoa mixture, stirring until smooth.

Per Serving

calories: 99 | fat: 1g | protein: 9g | carbs: 16g | fiber: 2g | sugar: 13g | sodium: 104mg

Berry Blast Protein Shake

Prep time: 5 minutes | Cook time: 0 minutes | Serves 2

1 cup low-fat milk or unsweetened soy milk
¾ cup mixed frozen berries

1 scoop (¼ cup) vanilla or plain protein powder
5 ice cubes

1. In a blender, combine the milk, berries, protein powder, and ice cubes. Blend on high speed for 3 to 4 minutes, until the powder is well dissolved and no longer visible. 2. Pour half the shake into a glass and enjoy. 3. Refrigerate any shake you don't drink or use right away in an airtight container for up to 1 week. Reblend prior to serving.

Per Serving (1 cup)

calories: 126 | fat: 1g | protein: 15g | carbs: 14g | fiber: 3g | sugar: 10g | sodium: 153mg

Vanilla Apple Pie Protein Shake

Prep time: 5 minutes | Cook time: 0 minutes | Serves 2

1 cup low-fat milk
1 scoop (¼ cup) vanilla protein powder
1 small apple, peeled, cored, and chopped

1 teaspoon vanilla extract
2 teaspoons ground cinnamon
½ teaspoon ground nutmeg
5 ice cubes

1. In a blender, combine the milk, protein powder, apple, vanilla, cinnamon, nutmeg, and ice cubes. Blend on high speed for 3 to 4 minutes, until the powder is well dissolved and no longer visible. 2. Pour half the shake into a glass and enjoy. 3. Refrigerate any shake you don't drink or use right away in an airtight container for up to 1 week. Reblend prior to serving.

Per Serving (1 cup)

calories: 123 | fat: 1g | protein: 14g | carbs: 1g | fiber: 1g | sugar: 12g | sodium: 153mg

Black-and-White Peanut Butter Shake

Prep time: 5 minutes | Cook time: 0 minutes | Serves 4

4 cups unsweetened almond milk
4 scoops vanilla protein powder
4 tablespoons powered peanut butter

2 tablespoons cocoa powder
1 cup frozen cauliflower
1 cup ice (optional)

1. In a blender, combine the almond milk, protein powder, powdered peanut butter, and cocoa powder and blend until smooth. Add the cauliflower and blend again until smooth. Serve over ice (if using) or blend the ice into the shake to achieve your desired consistency. Serve immediately.

Per Serving

calories: 185 | fat: 5g | protein: 29g | carbs: 8g | fiber: 3g | sugar: 1g | sodium: 384mg

Banana-Chocolate Shake

Prep time: 5 minutes | Cook time: 0 minutes | Serves 4

3 cups skim milk
4 scoops chocolate protein powder
1 large very ripe banana

1 cup frozen cauliflower
1 cup ice
1 tablespoon ground cinnamon

1. In a blender or food processor, combine the milk and protein powder and blend to combine. Add the banana, cauliflower, ice, and cinnamon and blend again until smooth. Enjoy immediately.

Per Serving

calories: 209 | fat: 1g | protein: 32g | carbs: 19g | fiber: 2g | sugar: 14g | sodium: 234mg

Chicken Broth

Prep time: 15 minutes | Cook time: 2 hours | Serves 8

1 whole chicken (about 4 pounds / 1.8 kg)
2 quarts cold water, plus more as needed
2 carrots, cut into 2-inch pieces
2 celery stalks, cut into 2-inch pieces
1 onion, peeled and quartered

1 garlic clove, sliced
2 bay leaves
Fresh herb sprigs (optional)
Salt and freshly ground black pepper, to taste

1. Remove neck and giblets from chicken and discard or save for another use. Rinse chicken and place in a large stockpot. 2. Add remaining ingredients to pot, adding more water if needed to fully submerge ingredients. Season broth mixture to taste with salt and pepper. 3. Heat broth mixture to a boil, skimming foam as necessary. Reduce heat, cover pot and simmer until chicken is cooked through and tender, 1½ to 2 hours. 4. Remove chicken from pot and let cool. Remove and discard chicken skin and bones and chop or shred meat. Serve meat immediately as desired or save for later use. 5. Strain broth through a fine sieve and discard solids. Serve broth immediately as desired or save for later use. Enjoy!

Per Serving

calories: 346 | fat: 18g | protein: 40g | carbs: 5g | fiber: 1g | sugar: 3g | sodium: 153mg

Tomato Soup

Prep time: 10 minutes | Cook time: 35 minutes | Serves 6

1 tablespoon olive oil
1 yellow onion, coarsely diced
2 garlic cloves, minced
Dash of red pepper flakes

1 can (28-ounce / 794-g) whole peeled tomatoes, undrained
1 teaspoon dried basil
2 cups chicken broth or water
2 cups skim milk

1. In a medium saucepan, heat olive over medium-low heat and sauté onion until softened, about 5 minutes, stirring occasionally. Add garlic and red pepper flakes and sauté for 1 minute more, stirring constantly. 2. Add tomatoes and basil to pan and increase heat to medium-high. Crush tomatoes with a spoon and cook for about 10 minutes, stirring occasionally. Add broth to pan and simmer until tomatoes are falling apart, about 15 minutes. 3. Remove pan from heat and let soup cool briefly. Carefully purée soup with an immersion blender until smooth. 4. Reheat soup over medium heat, add milk and stir until heated through. Serve immediately and enjoy!

Per Serving

calories: 106 | fat: 4g | protein: 8g | carbs: 11g | fiber: 3g | sugar: 8g | sodium: 312mg

Chapter 5 Puréed Foods

20	Sunny Orange Smoothie	28
21	Cheery Cherry Smoothie	28
22	Fruit Smoothies with Kale	28
23	Pumpkin Curry Soup	28
24	Swiss Chard Soup	29
25	Savory Eggplant Purée	29
26	Pumpkin Cheesecake Mousse	29
27	Sweet Chia Pudding	30
28	Broccoli-Cheddar Purée	30
29	Strawberry Dream Cream Shake	30
30	Roasted Carrot Purée	30
31	Sweet Potato, Ginger, and Carrot Soup	31
32	Butternut Squash and Black Bean Soup	31
33	Cheese Pizza Purée	31
34	Harvest Vegetable Chicken Purée	32
35	Cheesy Cauliflower Casserole	32
36	Creamy Harvest Oatmeal	32
37	Sweet Cinnamon-Vanilla Ricotta Cheese	33
38	Ricotta Scrambled Eggs	33
39	Deviled Chicken Spread	33
40	Garlic-Parmesan Cauliflower Mash	33

Sunny Orange Smoothie

Prep time: 5 minutes | Cook time: 0 minutes | Serves 1

½ cup vanilla frozen yogurt
½ cup skim milk

½ teaspoon orange extract

1. Place all ingredients in a blender container and pulse until smooth. Serve immediately and enjoy!

Per Serving

calories: 159 | fat: 4g | protein: 7g | carbs: 24g | fiber: 30g | sugar: 12g | sodium: 127mg

Cheery Cherry Smoothie

Prep time: 5 minutes | Cook time: 0 minutes | Serves 1

1 cup ice cubes
½ cup water
½ cup frozen bing cherries

1 serving (about 2 tablespoons) vanilla-flavored or fruit-flavored low-carb whey or soy protein isolate powder

1. Place all ingredients in a blender container and pulse until smooth. Serve immediately and enjoy!

Per Serving

calories: 159 | fat: 0g | protein: 33g | carbs: 12g | fiber: 2g | sugar: 9g | sodium: 20mg

Fruit Smoothies with Kale

Prep time: 10 minutes | Cook time: 0 minutes | Serves 2

1 apple, peeled, cored, diced
½ cup chopped kale

½ cup blackberries
6 to 8 ice cubes

1. Place all ingredients in a blender container and pulse until smooth. Serve immediately and enjoy!

Per Serving

calories: 65 | fat: 0g | protein: 1g | carbs: 16g | fiber: 4g | sugar: 2g | sodium: 3mg

Pumpkin Curry Soup

Prep time: 15 minutes | Cook time: 20 minutes | Serves 4

1 tablespoon butter
4 scallions, chopped
2 fresh red chili peppers, minced
2 garlic cloves, minced
3 cups chicken stock

2 cups fresh or canned pumpkin purée
1 cup unsweetened coconut milk
2 teaspoons curry powder, plus more to taste
Salt and freshly ground black pepper, to taste
2 tablespoons sour cream
1 tablespoon skim milk

1. In a medium saucepan, melt butter over medium heat and sauté scallions and chili peppers until softened, about 5 minutes, stirring occasionally. Add garlic and sauté about 1 minute more, stirring constantly. 2. Add chicken stock, pumpkin, coconut milk and curry powder to pan and season to taste with salt and pepper. and stir until thoroughly combined. Heat soup to a boil, stirring occasionally. 3. If necessary, purée soup with an immersion blender until smooth or to desired consistency. 4. Whisk sour cream and skim milk until smooth. Ladle soup into bowls and garnish each serving as desired with sour cream mixture. Serve and enjoy!

Per Serving

calories: 246 | fat: 19g | protein: 8g | carbs: 16g | fiber: 4g | sugar: 6g | sodium: 76mg

Swiss Chard Soup

Prep time: 20 minutes | Cook time: 15 minutes | Serves 4

3 cups chicken stock
1 bunch Swiss chard, chopped
1 small head cauliflower, cut into florets
1 cup skim milk
1 tablespoon balsamic vinegar

1 teaspoon garlic powder
1 teaspoon onion powder
Salt and freshly ground black pepper, to taste
4 tablespoons finely grated Parmesan cheese

1. Pour chicken stock into a medium saucepan and add chard and cauliflower. Heat mixture to a boil, stirring occasionally. Reduce heat, cover and simmer until cauliflower is very soft, about 10 minutes. 2. Add milk, balsamic vinegar, garlic powder and onion powder to soup. Season soup to taste with salt and pepper and purée to desired consistency with an immersion blender. 3. Ladle soup into bowls and sprinkle with Parmesan cheese to serve. Enjoy!

Per Serving
calories: 80 | fat: 2g | protein: 6g | carbs: 10g | fiber: 2g | sugar: 6g | sodium: 415mg

Savory Eggplant Purée

Prep time: 25 minutes | Cook time: 40 minutes | Serves 6

1 large eggplant
1 tablespoon olive oil
Salt and freshly ground black pepper, to taste
1 tablespoon butter

1 onion, diced
1 bell pepper, diced
1 garlic clove, minced
½ cup chicken broth, plus more as needed

1. Preheat oven to 400°F (205°C). Line a rimmed baking sheet with parchment paper. 2. Cut eggplant into quarters lengthwise and cut each quarter into 4 wedges. Brush eggplant flesh with olive oil and season to taste with salt and pepper. Place eggplant wedges skin-side down on prepared baking sheet and roast until golden brown, 25 to 30 minutes. Remove eggplant from oven and let cool. 3. While the eggplant is roasting, melt butter in a medium nonstick skillet and sauté onion and bell pepper until softened and golden brown, 7 to 8 minutes, stirring occasionally. Add garlic and sauté about 1 minute more, stirring constantly. Remove onion mixture from heat and let cool. 4. Cut skin from eggplant wedges discard. Cut eggplant flesh into 1-inch cubes. Place about 1 cup eggplant cubes, half of the onion mixture and ¼ cup broth in a food processor and pulse until smooth. Add more broth if needed to reach desired consistency. Repeat with remaining eggplant cubes and onion mixture. 5. Eggplant purée can be served immediately. Or, divide eggplant purée into ½-cup portions in zip-top plastic bags or tightly covered containers, and store in the refrigerator for up to 4 days or in the freezer for up to 2 weeks. Reheat cold eggplant purée in the microwave before serving. Enjoy!

Per Serving
calories: 74 | fat: 4g | protein: 1g | carbs:8 g | fiber: 3g | sugar: 4g | sodium: 89mg

Pumpkin Cheesecake Mousse

Prep time: 15 minutes | Cook time: 0 minutes | Serves 4

1 (3-ounce / 85-g) package cream cheese, softened
⅓ cup canned or fresh pumpkin purée
½ cup heavy cream

½ teaspoon pumpkin pie spice, plus more for garnish
¼ teaspoon vanilla extract
Dash salt

1. In a medium bowl, beat cream cheese and pumpkin with an electric hand mixer until smooth. 2. Add cream, spice, vanilla and salt and beat until light and fluffy, about 5 minutes. 3. Pipe or spoon mousse into 4 serving bowls or glasses and refrigerate until firm and set, about 1 hour. Sprinkle with a dash of pie spice just before serving. Enjoy!

Per Serving
calories: 131 | fat: 13g | protein: 2g | carbs: 3g | fiber: 1g | sugar: 2g | sodium: 186mg

Sweet Chia Pudding

Prep time: 5 minutes | Cook time: 0 minutes | Serves 4

2 cups unsweetened almond milk
1 cup plain nonfat Greek yogurt
½ cup chia seeds
¼ cup maple syrup
1 tablespoon ground cinnamon
Fresh fruit or nuts, for serving (optional)

1. In a medium bowl, whisk together the almond milk and yogurt. 2. Add the chia seeds, maple syrup, and cinnamon to the milk mixture and mix very well to combine. 3. Allow the pudding to set, covered in the refrigerator, for about 2 hours or longer if time allows. 4. Mix just prior to serving and enjoy cold.

Per Serving
calories: 226 | fat: 8g | protein: 12g | carbs: 28g | fiber: 11g | sugar: 14g | sodium: 121mg

Broccoli-Cheddar Purée

Prep time: 5 minutes | Cook time: 5 minutes | Serves 4

2 cups diced broccoli florets
⅔ cup low-fat cottage cheese
⅓ cup part-skim shredded Cheddar cheese

1. Fill the bottom of a medium saucepan with a couple inches of water and insert a steamer basket. Place the broccoli in the steamer basket and bring the water to a boil. Cover and steam for 5 minutes or until tender. Remove from the heat. 2. Add the broccoli, cottage cheese, and Cheddar cheese to a blender or food processor. Blend the mixture for about 2 minutes or until smooth. Enjoy. 3. Store the leftover purée in an airtight container in the refrigerator for up to 5 days.

Per Serving (¾ cup)
calories: 78 | fat: 3g | protein: 8g | carbs: 7g | fiber: 2g | sugar: 3g | sodium: 185mg

Strawberry Dream Cream Shake

Prep time: 5 minutes | Cook time: 0 minutes | Serves 1

½ cup low-fat plain cottage cheese
3 tablespoons low-fat milk
6 frozen strawberries
Granulated sweetener, to taste

1. Place the cottage cheese, milk, strawberries, and sweetener to taste in a blender or food processor and blend until smooth. 2. Pour into a glass to serve.

Per Serving
calories: 113 | fat: 2g | protein: 15g | carbs: 10g | fiber: 2g | sugar: 7g | sodium: 85mg

Roasted Carrot Purée

Prep time: 5 minutes | Cook time: 30 minutes | Serves 4

1 cup peeled, sliced carrot
½ tablespoon extra-virgin olive oil
Dash salt
¾ cup nonfat plain Greek yogurt
¼ cup unsweetened almond milk

1. Preheat the oven to 425°F (220°C). Line a baking sheet with parchment paper and set aside. 2. In a bowl, toss the carrot and oil. Arrange the carrot slices on the prepared baking sheet and sprinkle with salt. 3. Bake for 25 to 30 minutes, until the carrot softens and starts to turn golden brown. 4. Add the carrot, yogurt, and almond milk to a blender. Blend on low for about a minute or so, until the mixture turns bright orange. Enjoy. 5. Store the leftover purée in an airtight container in the refrigerator for up to 5 days.

Per Serving (3½ tablespoons)
calories: 44 | fat: 2g | protein: 4g | carbs: 3g | fiber: 1g | sugar: 2g | sodium: 75mg

Sweet Potato, Ginger, and Carrot Soup

Prep time: 10 minutes | Cook time: 50 minutes | Serves 6

Low-fat cooking spray
2 pounds (907 g) sweet potatoes, peeled and chopped
1 pound (454 g) carrots, peeled and chopped
1 (1-inch) piece ginger, peeled and grated
1 teaspoon ground cumin

6 cups vegetable stock
Salt and freshly ground black pepper
Fat-free plain yogurt, snipped fresh chives, and grated carrot, for garnish (optional)

1. Generously spray a large nonstick pan with low-fat cooking spray. Heat, add the sweet potatoes, carrots, ginger, and cumin, and cook over high heat for about 10 minutes, stirring occasionally, until starting to brown. 2. Add the stock and salt and pepper, bring to a boil, cover, reduce heat, and simmer for about 40 minutes, until the vegetables are tender. 3. Purée in a blender until smooth. Return to the pan and reheat until hot. 4. Ladle into warmed bowls or cups and top with a swirl of plain yogurt, a sprinkling of chives, and a little grated carrot, if desired.

Per Serving
calories: 329 | fat: 5g | protein: 15g | carbs: 59g | fiber: 8g | sugar: 13g | sodium: 220mg

Butternut Squash and Black Bean Soup

Prep time: 10 minutes | Cook time: 30 minutes | Serves 4

1 (1-pound / 454-g) butternut squash, peeled and diced
1 medium red onion, quartered
6 garlic cloves, peeled and halved
1 tablespoon plus 2 teaspoons extra-virgin olive oil

Salt
Freshly ground black pepper
1 (32-ounce / 907-g) container low-sodium vegetable stock
1 (15½-ounce / 439-g) can black beans, drained and rinsed

1. Preheat the oven to 400ºF (205ºC). 2. On a baking sheet, place the butternut squash, onion, and garlic and toss with the olive oil. Season with salt and pepper, then roast for about 20 minutes, until the vegetables are very soft and the squash is golden brown. 3. While the vegetables are roasting, in a large stockpot over medium heat, warm the vegetable stock and black beans. 4. Remove the roasted squash from the oven and add to it the stock and beans. Cook for about 5 minutes, until simmering. 5. Remove from the heat and then use an immersion blender to purée the soup or, working in batches, use a blender or food processor to blend until smooth. 6. Return the soup to medium heat and warm for about 5 minutes to let the flavors meld. Season with salt and pepper. Serve immediately.

Per Serving
calories: 204 | fat: 6g | protein: 7g | carbs: 30g | fiber: 7g | sugar: 4g | sodium: 79mg

Cheese Pizza Purée

Prep time: 5 minutes | Cook time: 5 minutes | Serves 4

½ cup unsweetened almond milk
1 tablespoon cornstarch
1 cup part-skim shredded Mozzarella cheese

1 cup canned diced tomatoes, drained
Dash salt

1. In a medium saucepan, heat the almond milk over medium heat. Whisk in the cornstarch and bring the mixture to a rolling boil. 2. Reduce the heat to low-medium and mix in the Mozzarella cheese a few tablespoons at a time, stirring continuously. 3. Once the cheese is melted and combined with the milk, remove the pan from the heat and set aside to cool slightly. 4. Place the tomato and salt in a blender and blend on low for about 30 seconds or until smooth. 5. In a large serving bowl, combine the cheese and tomato mixtures and enjoy. 6. Store leftovers in an airtight container in the refrigerator for 3 to 4 days.

Per Serving (7 tablespoons)
calories: 104 | fat: 6g | protein: 8g | carbs: 6g | fiber: 1g | sugar: 2g | sodium: 321mg

Harvest Vegetable Chicken Purée

Prep time: 5 minutes | Cook time: 25 minutes | Serves 4

1 tablespoon extra-virgin olive oil
2 cups peeled, thinly sliced carrot
½ cup diced yellow onion

1 cup shredded chicken breast
1 cup chicken broth
¼ teaspoon salt

1. In a large saucepan, heat the oil over medium-high heat. Add the carrot and onion to the pan and cook, stirring every 30 seconds or so, for 7 to 9 minutes, or until the onion is translucent and the carrot is soft. Add a few tablespoons of water if needed to help steam carrot. 2. Add the chicken, broth, and salt to the pan. Simmer for another 7 to 9 minutes on low heat to allow the flavors to develop. 3. Turn off the heat and remove the pan from burner. Allow mixture to cool for 5 to 7 minutes. 4. Place the cooled mixture in a blender or food processor. Blend on low for about 2 minutes or until smooth. Enjoy. 5. Store leftovers in an airtight container in the refrigerator for 5 to 7 days.

Per Serving (½ cup)
calories: 171 | fat: 6g | protein: 19g | carbs: 6g | fiber: 1g | sugar: 3g | sodium: 247mg

Cheesy Cauliflower Casserole

Prep time: 10 minutes | Cook time: 45 minutes | Serves 8

1 head cauliflower, cut into florets
1 cup low-fat cottage cheese
1 cup low-fat plain Greek yogurt
½ teaspoon Dijon mustard

¼ teaspoon garlic powder
2 ounces (57 g) shredded aged white Cheddar cheese
2 ounces (57 g) shredded mild Cheddar cheese

1. Preheat the oven to 350°F (180°C). 2. Fill a medium pot one-third full with water, and place a steamer basket inside. Bring the water to a boil over high heat. 3. Add the cauliflower to the steamer basket, cover the pot, and reduce the heat to a gentle boil. Steam the cauliflower for 10 to 15 minutes, or until the florets are soft. Alternatively, you can steam the cauliflower with 2 tablespoons of water in the microwave on high for about 4 minutes, or until tender. 4. While the cauliflower steams, mix together the cottage cheese, yogurt, mustard, and garlic powder in a medium bowl. 5. Drain the cauliflower in a large colander, and gently mash it with a potato masher to drain out excess water. 6. Stir the cauliflower pieces into the cottage cheese mixture. Add the Cheddar cheeses and mix well. 7. Transfer the cauliflower mixture to an 8-by-8-inch or 11-by-7-inch baking dish. Bake for about 30 minutes. It is done when the edges begin to brown. 8. Serve immediately.

Per Serving (½ cup)
calories: 147 | fat: 7g | protein: 13g | carbs: g | fiber: 8g | sugar: 4g | sodium: 263mg

Creamy Harvest Oatmeal

Prep time: 5 minutes | Cook time: 10 minutes | Serves 4

2½ cups unsweetened almond milk
1 cup old-fashioned rolled oats
1 tablespoon ground cinnamon, plus more for garnish

1 cup whipped low-fat cottage cheese
½ cup unsweetened applesauce

1. In a medium saucepan over medium heat, warm the almond milk, oats, and cinnamon. Cook, stirring periodically, until the oats are cooked and the oatmeal has thickened, about 10 minutes or more, depending on your desired texture. 2. Once the oat mixture is thickened to your liking, remove it from the heat and add the cottage cheese and applesauce, stirring well to combine. 3. Serve immediately, garnished with more cinnamon as desired.

Per Serving
calories: 162 | fat: 7g | protein: 9g | carbs: 22g | fiber: 4g | sugar: 5g | sodium: 304mg

Sweet Cinnamon-Vanilla Ricotta Cheese

Prep time: 5 minutes | Cook time: 0 minutes | Serves 2

1 cup low-fat ricotta cheese
1 teaspoon vanilla extract

1 teaspoon ground cinnamon
1 teaspoon ground nutmeg
½ teaspoon powdered stevia extract

1. In a small container with an airtight lid, use a spoon to mix the ricotta cheese, vanilla, cinnamon, nutmeg, and stevia for 1 minute, until the spices are well distributed among the ricotta cheese. 2. Serve right away or refrigerate overnight for even better flavor.

Per Serving (½ cup)
calories: 116 | fat: 5g | protein: 13g | carbs: 6g | fiber: 0g | sugar: 4g | sodium: 140mg

Ricotta Scrambled Eggs

Prep time: 5 minutes | Cook time: 10 minutes | Serves 4

8 large eggs
¼ cup skim milk
2 tablespoons low-fat ricotta cheese

1 teaspoon extra-virgin olive oil
Salt
Freshly ground black pepper

1. In a small bowl, beat the eggs, milk, and ricotta cheese very well until combined. 2. In a nonstick skillet over very low heat, warm the olive oil. Add the egg mixture and let it sit, undisturbed, for 30 seconds. 3. With a rubber spatula, stir intermittently until the eggs are just set and no raw whites are visible, about 5 minutes, or until they are set to your liking. 4. Season with salt and pepper and serve immediately.

Per Serving
calories: 170 | fat: 11g | protein: 14g | carbs: 2g | fiber: 0g | sugar: 1g | sodium: 158mg

Deviled Chicken Spread

Prep time: 5 minutes | Cook time: 0 minutes | Serves 4

1 cup cubed cooked chicken breast
½ cup low-fat mayonnaise
2 tablespoons Dijon mustard

⅓ cup coarsely chopped sweet onion
2 tablespoons paprika
1 teaspoon lemon-pepper
½ teaspoon chili powder, or to taste

1. In bowl of a food processor, combine chicken and mayonnaise and purée until smooth. 2. Add all other ingredients and purée until very smooth.

Per Serving
calories: 133 | fat: 6g | protein: 17g | carbs: 5g | fiber: 2g | sugar: 2g | sodium: 254mg

Garlic-Parmesan Cauliflower Mash

Prep time: 15 minutes | Cook time: 10 minutes | Serves 2

4 cups cauliflower florets
1 teaspoon extra-virgin olive oil
3 garlic cloves, minced

⅓ cup grated Parmesan cheese
1 tablespoon low-fat cream cheese
½ teaspoon salt

1. In a large pot, bring ¼ cup of water to a boil. Add the cauliflower florets. Cook, covered, for 3 to 8 minutes, or until fork tender. Drain and discard the steaming liquid. 2. In a small skillet over medium heat, heat the oil. Add the garlic, and sauté until aromatic, 1 to 2 minutes. 3. In a food processor or high-speed blender, blend the cauliflower, garlic, cheeses, and salt until smooth. Serve warm.

Per Serving
calories: 169 | fat: 9g | protein: 12g | carbs: 13g | fiber: 5g | sugar: 4g | sodium: 628mg

Chapter 6 Soft Foods

41   Mushroom Soup with Brie   35

42   Lemon Avocado Soup   35

43   Southwestern Squash Soup   35

44   Scrambled Eggs with Ham and Cheese   36

45   Omelet Italiano   36

46   PB and J Overnight No-Oats Cereal   36

47   Porridge with Berries   37

48   Pizza Casserole   37

49   Crustless Spinach Quiche   37

50   Banana Brûlée Yogurt Parfait   38

51   Tofu Scramble   38

52   Cashew Pork with Ginger Green Beans   38

53   Lemon Soufflé   39

54   Lemon-Dijon Tuna Salad   39

55   Basic Cheesecake   39

56   10-Clove Garlic Shrimp   40

57   Hoisin and Soy Beef   40

58   Tempeh-and-Parmesan Risotto   40

59   Beef Stew   41

60   Sloppy Joe–Style Ground Pork   41

61   Healthier Fudge Brownies   41

Mushroom Soup with Brie

Prep time: 15 minutes | Cook time: 30 minutes | Serves 6

2 tablespoons butter
2 (8-ounce / 227-g) packages baby bella mushrooms, sliced
1 onion, julienned
2 garlic cloves, minced
1 teaspoon dried thyme

½ cup white wine
2 tablespoons flour
3 cups chicken stock
3 cups skim milk
4 ounces (113 g) Brie, rind removed as necessary

1. Melt butter in a large saucepan and sauté mushrooms and onion until softened and caramelized, 8 to 10 minutes, stirring frequently. Add garlic and thyme sauté about 1 minute more, stirring constantly. Add wine and stir to deglaze pan. 2. Sprinkle flour into saucepan and stir to coat. Add broth and heat to a boil, stirring occasionally. Reduce heat and simmer soup for about 10 minutes, stirring occasionally. 3. Add milk to soup and heat to a simmer. Stir Brie into soup and stir until melted. Remove soup from heat and process with an immersion blender to desired consistency. Serve immediately and enjoy!

Per Serving
calories: 194 | fat: 10g | protein: 13g | carbs: 14g | fiber: 1g | sugar: 9g | sodium: 213mg

Lemon Avocado Soup

Prep time: 15 minutes | Cook time: 0 minutes | Serves 4

2 avocados, pitted, peeled, and diced
1 small onion, diced
2 garlic cloves, minced
2 tablespoons chopped chipotles in adobo sauce
1½ cups plain unsweetened Greek yogurt

¾ cup skim milk, plus more as needed
1 lemon, zested and juiced
1 teaspoon ground cumin
1 teaspoon kosher salt, plus more to taste
Chili powder, for garnish

1. Pulse avocados, onion, garlic and chipotles in a food processor until thoroughly combined. Add yogurt, milk, lemon juice, cumin and salt and process until smooth. Add milk as necessary to achieve desired consistency. 2. Refrigerate soup until chilled through, about 1 hour. 3. Ladle soup into 4 bowls and sprinkle with lemon zest and chili powder to serve. Enjoy!

Per Serving
calories: 245 | fat: 15g | protein: 9g | carbs: 22g | fiber: 7g | sugar: 11g | sodium: 648mg

Southwestern Squash Soup

Prep time: 20 minutes | Cook time: 35 minutes | Serves 6

2 tablespoons olive oil
1 medium leek, white portion only, diced
1 white onion, diced
1 jalapeño pepper, seeded, diced
4 garlic cloves, minced
6 medium yellow summer squash, seeded and cubed
4 cups chicken stock

2 tablespoons lemon juice
1 teaspoon hot sauce, plus more to taste
1 teaspoon ground cumin
1 teaspoon dried oregano
1 teaspoon kosher salt, plus more to taste
¼ teaspoon cayenne pepper, plus more to taste
½ cup toasted pumpkin seeds
Chili powder, for garnish

1. Heat oil in a large saucepan over medium heat and sauté leek, onion and jalapeño until softened, about 5 minutes, stirring occasionally. Add squash and sauté for about 5 minutes, stirring occasionally. Add garlic and sauté about 1 minute more, stirring constantly. 2. Add chicken stock, lemon juice, hot sauce, cumin, oregano, salt and cayenne pepper to pan and stir to combine and heat to a boil. Reduce heat and simmer, uncovered, for about 20 minutes. 3. Purée soup with an immersion blender until smooth. Ladle soup into bowls and garnish with pumpkin seeds and chili powder to serve. Enjoy!

Per Serving
calories: 179 | fat: 11g | protein: 7g | carbs: 16g | fiber: 4g | sugar: 6g | sodium: 453mg

Scrambled Eggs with Ham and Cheese

Prep time: 5 minutes | Cook time: 2 minutes | Serves 4

1 cup egg substitute
1 tablespoon water
4 ounces (113 g) low-fat Cheddar cheese, diced
4 ounces (113 g) low-fat sliced ham, finely minced
Butter-flavored cooking spray
Salt and pepper, to taste

1. In a small bowl, beat egg substitute with water until frothy. Stir in cheese and ham. 2. In a medium nonstick skillet, heat cooking spray over medium heat until hot but not smoking. Pour in egg mixture, stirring constantly for 1 to 2 minutes, or until eggs form small curds that are soft but not runny and cheese melts. Add salt and pepper to taste.

Per Serving
calories: 146 | fat: 7g | protein: 19g | carbs: 2g | fiber: 0g | sugar: 1g | sodium: 503mg

Omelet Italiano

Prep time: 10 minutes | Cook time: 9 minutes | Serves 4

Butter-flavored cooking spray
2 low-fat turkey sausages (sweet Italian-style)
8 to 10 fresh mushrooms, thinly sliced
½ cup chopped onion
1 cup chopped ripe plum tomatoes
2 teaspoons dried basil
1 cup egg substitute
4 teaspoons water
4 ounces (113 g) grated part-skim Mozzarella cheese
Salt and pepper, to taste

1. In a large nonstick lidded skillet, heat cooking spray over medium heat until hot but not smoking. While skillet is heating, remove sausage meat from casings; then brown it, breaking up lumps, for 2 minutes. 2. Add mushrooms and onion and brown them, stirring, for 2 minutes. 3. Stir in tomatoes and basil, lower heat, and cook, covered, for 3 minutes, or until tomatoes are softened. 4. Remove sausage-tomato mixture from skillet and keep warm. Make Each Omelet: 5. In a small bowl, combine ¼ cup egg substitute with 1 teaspoon water and beat well. 6. Heat medium lidded skillet over medium heat until hot but not smoking. Pour in egg substitute and swirl pan until entire bottom is covered. Place 1 ounce (28 g) cheese on one half of egg and top with 3 tablespoons of sausage mixture. 7. Fold other side of omelet over filling, lower heat, and cook, covered, for 2 minutes, or until cheese melts. 8. Slide omelet onto plate and keep warm. Re-spray pan and repeat for all remaining omelets. Add salt and pepper to taste.

Per Serving
calories: 144 | fat: 3g | protein: 22g | carbs: 9g | fiber: 3g | sugar: 5g | sodium: 407mg

PB and J Overnight No-Oats Cereal

Prep time: 5 minutes | Cook time: 2 minutes | Serves 2

1 cup nonfat plain Greek yogurt
6 tablespoons almond flour
1 tablespoon chia seeds
1 tablespoon unsweetened peanut butter powder
¼ teaspoon stevia
¼ cup diced fresh or frozen strawberries

1. In a pint-size canning jar, mix the yogurt, almond flour, chia seeds, peanut butter powder, and stevia. Set aside. 2. Heat a small skillet over medium heat. Place the strawberries in the skillet. Cook on medium heat for 1 to 2 minutes until the strawberries soften. 3. Pour the strawberries into the jar and mix well with other ingredients. Seal the jar tightly and place in the refrigerator. Allow the mixture to sit overnight for at least 8 hours to set. 4. Scoop out ½ cup of the mixture if you're only eating one serving. Enjoy cold or heat in the microwave for about 30 seconds or so to warm before eating. 5. Store in a microwave-safe container so you can heat it up safely before enjoying. Store refrigerated for up to 3 days.

Per Serving (½ cup)
calories: 232 | fat: 13g | protein: 19g | carbs: 14g | fiber: 8g | sugar: 6g | sodium: 45mg

Porridge with Berries

Prep time: 5 minutes | Cook time: 10 minutes | Serves 2

1 cup water
1 cup frozen mixed berries
1 tablespoon lemon juice

3 tablespoons farina breakfast porridge mix (such as Cream of Wheat or Malt-O-Meal)

1. Mix water, berries and lemon juice in a small saucepan and heat to a boil over medium heat, stirring occasionally, gently crushing berries to desired consistency. 2. Whisk farina into saucepan and stir until smooth. 3. Reduce heat and simmer, uncovered, until porridge is thickened, about 2 minutes, stirring occasionally. Serve immediately and enjoy!

Per Serving
calories: 95 | fat: 0g | protein: 3g | carbs: 20g | fiber: 4g | sugar: 5g | sodium: 38mg

Pizza Casserole

Prep time: 30 minutes | Cook time: 35 minutes | Serves 6

1 medium head cauliflower, cored, cut into florets
4 ounces (113 g) Italian pork sausage
4 ounces (113 g) pepperoni slices
1 cup spaghetti sauce
1 teaspoon Italian herb blend
½ cup shredded mozzarella cheese
¼ cup grated Parmesan cheese

1. Preheat oven to 400ºF (205ºC). Spray a glass 8 x 8 inch baking pan with nonstick cooking spray and set aside. 2. Pour water into a large saucepan to a depth of about 2 inches. Set steamer basket in saucepan and place cauliflower in basket. Cover pan and steam over medium heat until cauliflower is soft, 10 to 12 minutes. 3. Meanwhile, crumble sausage in a small nonstick skillet and sauté until browned and cooked through, about 5 minutes, stirring frequently. Drain fat from sausage as necessary and set aside. 4. Pulse cauliflower, sausage, pepperoni and about ¼ cup spaghetti sauce in a food processor until smooth. 5. Evenly spread cauliflower mixture in prepared baking pan. Evenly spread remaining spaghetti sauce over cauliflower mixture and sprinkle with Italian herbs and cheeses. 6. Bake casserole until cheese is melted and golden brown, about 20 minutes. Remove casserole from oven and let stand for about 5 minutes before serving. Enjoy!

Per Serving
calories: 235 | fat: 17g | protein: 13g | carbs: 9g | fiber: 3g | sugar: 4g | sodium: 358mg

Crustless Spinach Quiche

Prep time: 15 minutes | Cook time: 45 minutes | Serves 6

1 tablespoon butter
1 onion, diced
1 garlic clove, minced
1 (10-ounce / 283-g) package frozen chopped spinach, thawed, and drained
6 eggs, lightly beaten
1 cup Monterey Jack cheese
½ teaspoon kosher salt, plus more to taste
¼ teaspoon freshly ground black pepper, plus more to taste

1. Preheat oven to 350ºF (180ºC). Spray a glass 9 inch pie pan with nonstick cooking spray and set aside. 2. Melt butter in a small nonstick skillet over medium heat and onion until softened, about 5 minutes, stirring occasionally. Add garlic and sauté about 1 minute more, stirring constantly. Add spinach and cook until moisture is mostly evaporated, about 5 minutes, stirring occasionally. 3. In a large bowl, mix eggs, cheese, salt and pepper and stir to combine. Add spinach mixture and stir to thoroughly combine. 4. Evenly pour egg mixture into prepared pan and bake until eggs are cooked through and set, about 30 minutes. 5. Remove quiche from oven and let stand for about 10 minutes before slicing to serve. Enjoy!

Per Serving
calories: 157 | fat: 11g | protein: 10g | carbs: 4g | fiber: 1g | sugar: 1g | sodium: 631mg

Banana Brûlée Yogurt Parfait

Prep time: 5 minutes | Cook time: 2 minutes | Serves 1

Nonstick cooking spray
¼ cup banana slices
1 teaspoon brown sugar
1 cup nonfat plain Greek yogurt
Dash ground cinnamon

1. Spray a small skillet with cooking spray. Place over medium heat. 2. Place the banana slices in the skillet. Sprinkle the brown sugar over the banana slices. Cook for 1 to 2 minutes, stirring frequently, until heated through. Remove from the heat. 3. Place the yogurt into a bowl and pour the banana mixture over the yogurt. Sprinkle with cinnamon and enjoy immediately. 4. Store leftovers of the hash in an airtight container in the refrigerator for up to 3 days.

Per Serving (1¼ cups)

calories: 168 | fat:0 g | protein: 24g | carbs: 20g | fiber: 1g | sugar: 16g | sodium: 88mg

Tofu Scramble

Prep time: 5 minutes | Cook time: 10 minutes | Serves 4

4 teaspoons extra-virgin olive oil
¼ cup diced yellow onion
12 ounces (340 g) firm tofu, drained and cut into 1-inch squares
¼ teaspoon ground turmeric
¼ teaspoon garlic powder
¼ teaspoon salt
Freshly ground black pepper (optional)

1. In a medium skillet, heat the oil over medium heat. Add the onion and stir frequently for 5 minutes, or until the onion is translucent. 2. Add the tofu and use a mixing spoon to scramble the tofu into smaller pieces while combining with the onion. 3. Add the turmeric, garlic powder, salt, and pepper (if using) to taste. Continue to stir for 3 to 5 minutes to heat through. Serve warm. 3. Store leftovers in an airtight container in the refrigerator for up to 3 days.

Per Serving (½ cup)

calories: 115 | fat: 9g | protein: 7g | carbs: 3g | fiber: 2g | sugar: 1g | sodium: 156mg

Cashew Pork with Ginger Green Beans

Prep time: 10 minutes | Cook time: 20 minutes | Serves 4

2 tablespoons extra-virgin olive oil, divided
1 (12-ounce / 340-g) package green beans, trimmed and cut into bite-size pieces
2 tablespoons minced peeled fresh ginger
1 pound (454 g) extra-lean ground pork
6 garlic cloves, thinly sliced
⅓ cup chopped roasted salted cashews
Salt
Freshly ground black pepper

1. In a large nonstick skillet over medium-high heat, warm 1 tablespoon of olive oil. Add the green beans and ginger and cook for about 5 minutes, or until soft, fragrant, and just browned. Remove the green beans from the pan and set aside. 2. Turn the heat down to medium-low. In the same skillet, heat the remaining 1 tablespoon of olive oil. Add the pork and garlic and cook for about 10 minutes, breaking the pork up periodically, until totally cooked through and no pink remains. 3. Once the pork is fully cooked, add the beans back to the pork, toss to combine, and cook for another 5 minutes. 4. Add the cashews and toss to combine. Season with salt and pepper and serve.

Per Serving

calories: 310 | fat: 17g | protein: 28g | carbs: 12g | fiber: 3g | sugar: 3g | sodium: 108mg

Lemon Soufflé

Prep time: 5 minutes | Cook time: 35 minutes | Serves 4

2 large eggs, separated
2 tablespoons grated lemon zest
¼ cup fresh lemon juice

6 packets artificial sweetener (Splenda or Truvia)
1 (12-ounce / 340-g) can fat-free evaporated milk

1. Preheat oven to 350°F (180°C). 2. Beat egg whites until stiff. 3. In a separate bowl, mix all other ingredients together and gently fold in egg whites. 4. Pour into a 2-quart casserole or soufflé dish and place dish in a baking pan. Pour hot water into baking pan until it reaches halfway up sides of soufflé dish. 5. Bake for 35 minutes.

Per Serving
calories: 76 | fat: 3g | protein: 6g | carbs: 7g | fiber: 0g | sugar: 6g | sodium: 80mg

Lemon-Dijon Tuna Salad

Prep time: 5 minutes | Cook time: 0 minutes | Serves 4

2 (5-ounce / 142-g) cans water-packed tuna, drained
½ cup mayonnaise
2 teaspoons freshly squeezed lemon juice
1 teaspoon Dijon mustard

2 teaspoons dill pickle juice
Salt
Freshly ground black pepper

1. In a medium bowl, mash the tuna with a fork. 2. Add the mayonnaise, lemon juice, mustard, and pickle juice, and season with salt and pepper to taste. Mix until well combined, and serve.

Per Serving
calories: 227 | fat: 20g | protein: 10g | carbs: 5g | fiber: 0g | sugar: 3g | sodium: 384mg

Basic Cheesecake

Prep time: 15 minutes | Cook time: 30 minutes | Serves 8

1 (8-ounce / 227-g) container fat-free cream cheese
½ pound (227 g) silken tofu
½ cup egg substitute
6 packets artificial sweetener (Splenda or Truvia)
½ teaspoon vanilla extract

¼ teaspoon almond extract
6 tablespoons egg white substitute
¼ teaspoon cream of tartar
Butter-flavored cooking spray

1. Preheat oven to 350°F (180°C). 2. In a large bowl, using an electric mixer, beat together cream cheese, tofu, egg substitute, sweetener, vanilla, and almond extract until smooth and creamy. 3. In a small bowl, using an electric mixer, whip egg white substitute with cream of tartar until it forms stiff peaks. 4. Gently fold whipped egg whites into cream cheese mixture. 5. Coat a 8-inch square cake pan with cooking spray and pour in batter. Place cake pan into a baking pan and pour hot water into baking pan until it reaches halfway up sides of cake pan. Place in oven and bake for 30 minutes. 6. Remove from oven, let cool, then refrigerate for at least 4 hours.

Per Serving
calories: 82 | fat: 2g | protein: 13g | carbs: 4g | fiber: 0g | sugar: 3g | sodium: 296mg

10-Clove Garlic Shrimp

Prep time: 5 minutes | Cook time: 10 minutes | Serves 4

2 tablespoons extra-virgin olive oil
1 small white onion, diced
10 large garlic cloves, minced
1 pound (454 g) raw large shrimp, peeled and deveined
⅓ cup white wine
Pinch red pepper flakes, for garnish (optional)

1. In a large nonstick skillet over low heat, heat the olive oil. Sauté the onion and garlic for about 5 minutes, until fragrant and just golden brown. 2. Using a slotted spoon, remove the garlic and onion from the pan, leaving the oil. 3. Add the shrimp and white wine and cook for about 5 minutes, until just cooked, pink in color, and starting to curl. 4. Return the garlic and onion to the skillet and stir to combine. 5. Serve hot with the red pepper flakes (if using) sprinkled on top.

Per Serving
calories: 224 | fat: 9g | protein: 29g | carbs: 4g | fiber: 1g | sugar: 1g | sodium: 616mg

Hoisin and Soy Beef

Prep time: 5 minutes | Cook time: 20 minutes | Serves 4

1 pound (454 g) 95 percent lean ground beef
3 tablespoons hoisin sauce
2 tablespoons soy sauce
1 tablespoon seasoned rice vinegar
1 tablespoon sriracha or juice of 1 lime

1. Warm a large skillet or heavy bottomed pan over medium heat. Add the ground beef and cook for about 5 minutes, or until just beginning to brown. Use a spatula to break up the beef into smaller crumbles. 2. Add the hoisin, soy sauce, rice vinegar, and sriracha and stir well to combine. 3. Continue to stir the meat for about 15 minutes, or until the beef reaches an internal temperature of 160°F (71°C) and is no longer pink inside. Serve warm.

Per Serving
calories: 189 | fat: 5g | protein: 25g | carbs: 8g | fiber: 0g | sugar: 5g | sodium: 845mg

Tempeh-and-Parmesan Risotto

Prep time: 5 minutes | Cook time: 35 minutes | Serves 5

8 ounces (227 g) tempeh
½ cup water
½ cup diced onion
1 tablespoon unsalted butter
¼ teaspoon salt
1 cup unsweetened soymilk
½ cup nonfat plain Greek yogurt
1 cup shredded Parmesan cheese

1. In a medium saucepan, combine the tempeh and water and cook on medium heat for about 8 minutes, until softened. 2. Add the onion, butter, and salt and cook for 5 to 7 minutes, or until the onion is translucent. 3. Add the soymilk and yogurt to the pan. Bring to a rolling boil. Fold in the Parmesan cheese and cook for another 15 to 20 minutes on low-to-medium heat or until sauce thickens, stirring frequently. Remove from heat and serve. 4. Store leftovers in an airtight container in the refrigerator for up to 3 days.

Per Serving (½ cup)
calories: 243 | fat: 15g | protein: 21g | carbs: 8g | fiber: 2g | sugar: 1g | sodium: 466mg

Beef Stew

Prep time: 20 minutes | Cook time: 2 hours | Serves 4

2 tablespoons extra-virgin olive oil
1⅓ pounds (605 g) chuck roast, cut into 1-inch cubes
1 yellow onion, cut into 1-inch pieces
2 garlic cloves, minced
6 cups beef broth
1 dried bay leaf
1 teaspoon dried thyme
Salt
Freshly ground black pepper
3 celery stalks, chopped
1 large carrot, peeled and sliced

1. In a large, heavy-bottomed pan over medium-high heat, heat the olive oil. Add the meat, and sear in batches. 2. Add the onion and garlic, lower the heat to medium, and continue to cook until the onion is translucent, 3 to 5 minutes. 3. Add the broth, bay leaf, thyme, and salt and pepper to taste. 4. Bring the stew to a boil. Lower the heat to simmer, cover, and cook for 1 to 1½ hours. Add the celery and carrot halfway through cooking. 5. Remove the bay leaf before serving.

Per Serving
calories: 376 | fat: 18g | protein: 45g | carbs: 8g | fiber: 2g | sugar: 3g | sodium: 415mg

Sloppy Joe-Style Ground Pork

Prep time: 5 minutes | Cook time: 10 minutes | Serves 4

1 tablespoon extra-virgin olive oil
8 ounces (227 g) lean ground pork
1 cup chopped yellow onion
1 cup canned diced tomatoes, drained
1 tablespoon apple cider vinegar
1 tablespoon brown sugar
1 teaspoon salt

1. In a large skillet, heat the oil over medium heat. Cook the pork and onion for 7 to 9 minutes, stirring frequently, until cooked through. Remove the skillet from the heat and drain the fat from the pork. 2. Return the skillet to the heat and add the tomatoes, apple cider vinegar, brown sugar, and salt. Reduce the heat to medium low and simmer for 2 minutes. Serve and enjoy. 3. Store leftovers in an airtight container in the refrigerator for up to 3 days or freeze for up to 3 months.

Per Serving (½ cup)
calories: 172 | fat: 9g | protein: 13g | carbs: 10g | fiber: 2g | sugar: 6g | sodium: 287mg

Healthier Fudge Brownies

Prep time: 10 minutes | Cook time: 30 minutes | Makes 16 brownies

Nonstick cooking spray
1 (14½-ounce / 411-g) can black beans, drained and rinsed
3 eggs
3 tablespoons canola oil
¼ cup unsweetened cocoa powder
1 teaspoon vanilla extract
⅓ cup granulated sugar
1 teaspoon instant coffee (optional)
½ cup dark chocolate chips

1. Preheat the oven to 350ºF (180ºC). Coat an 8-by-8-inch square baking dish with cooking spray. 2. In a blender, blend to combine the black beans, eggs, canola oil, cocoa powder, vanilla, sugar, and coffee (if using) until smooth and lump free. 3. Pour the mixture into the baking dish, and sprinkle the chocolate chips on top. 4. Bake until the top is dry and the edges start to pull away from the sides of the pan, about 30 minutes. 5. Cut into 16 brownies and serve.

Per Serving (1 brownie)
calories: 124 | fat: 6g | protein: 4g | carbs: 16g | fiber: 5g | sugar: 7g | sodium: 18mg

Chapter 7 Breakfasts

62 Zucchini Frittata   43
63 Stuffed Omelet with Almonds   43
64 Cottage Cheese Pancakes   43
65 Huevos Rancheros   44
66 Taco Omelet   44
67 Apple Cinnamon Oatmeal   44
68 Nutty Crunch Porridge   45
69 Make-Ahead Breakfast Burritos   45
70 Pumpkin Spice Muffins   45
71 Smoked Salmon Breakfast Toast   46
72 Smoothie Bowl with Greek Yogurt and Fresh Berries   46
73 Southwestern Scrambled Egg Burritos   46
74 Breakfast Almond Freezer Pops   47
75 Clementine, Cranberry, and Pecan Bircher Muesli   47
76 Granola and Fruit Breakfast Tartlets   47
77 Veggie and Egg Breakfast Sizzle   48
78 Breakfast Scones   48
79 Protein Loaf   48
80 Savory Stuffed Crepes   49
81 Chicken Livers and Scrambled Eggs   49

Zucchini Frittata

Prep time: 10 minutes | Cook time: 10 minutes | Serves 2

2 teaspoons butter, divided
1 cup shredded zucchini
Salt and freshly ground black pepper, to taste
4 eggs, lightly beaten

2 tablespoons skim milk
¼ teaspoon garlic salt
¼ teaspoon onion powder
2 tablespoons shredded mild Cheddar cheese

1. In a medium nonstick skillet over medium heat, melt 1 teaspoon butter and sauté zucchini until softened and lightly browned, 4 to 5 minutes, stirring frequently. 2. Drain zucchini if necessary and season to taste with salt and pepper. Beat eggs with milk, garlic salt, onion powder and zucchini until combined. Melt remaining 1 teaspoon butter in skillet, add egg mixture and cook until partially set. Lift edges of cooked egg with a spatula, let uncooked egg run underneath and continue until top of frittata is set, about 4 minutes. 3. Carefully flip frittata and let cook until lightly browned, 3 to 4 minutes. Remove skillet from heat, sprinkle cheese over frittata and let stand until cheese is melted. 4. Cut frittata in half and serve immediately. Enjoy!

Per Serving
calories: 205 | fat: 15g | protein: 14g | carbs: 4g | fiber: 1g | sugar: 3g | sodium: 425mg

Stuffed Omelet with Almonds

Prep time: 5 minutes | Cook time: 15 minutes | Serves 2

2 tablespoons sliced almonds
4 eggs, lightly beaten
2 tablespoons skim milk

1 teaspoon butter
½ cup low-fat cottage cheese
Salt and freshly ground black pepper, to taste

1. In a medium dry nonstick skillet over medium heat, toast almonds until lightly browned, stirring occasionally, 4 to 5 minutes. Remove almonds from skillet and set aside. 2. Whisk eggs and milk until thoroughly combined and season to taste with salt and pepper. Melt butter in the same skillet and pour in eggs. When eggs begin to cook, gently lift the cooked edges and tilt skillet to allow uncooked eggs to flow underneath. Continue lifting and tilting all around until no uncooked eggs remain on top of the cooked portion. 3. Cover skillet and let cook until omelet is lightly browned on the bottom, 2 to 3 minutes. Carefully flip omelet and cook until lightly browned, 3 to 4 minutes. 4. Slide omelet out of pan onto a serving plate and season to taste with salt and pepper. Spread cottage cheese over half of the omelet and sprinkle with toasted almonds. Fold omelet over filling , cut in half and serve immediately. Enjoy!

Per Serving
calories: 237 | fat: 15g | protein: 21g | carbs: 5g | fiber: 1g | sugar: 2g | sodium: 488mg

Cottage Cheese Pancakes

Prep time: 10 minutes | Cook time: 10 minutes | Serves 4

1 cup low-fat cottage cheese
3 eggs, lightly beaten
1½ teaspoons vegetable oil

½ cup flour
½ teaspoon baking powder

1. For the batter, whisk cottage cheese, eggs and oil until thoroughly combined. Toss flour and baking powder and stir into cottage cheese mixture just until combined. 2. Spray a large nonstick skillet with cooking spray and heat over medium heat. Pour batter in ½ cup portions into skillet and fry until bubbly on top, 3 to 4 minutes. Flip pancakes and cook until browned and cooked through, 2 to 3 minutes more. 3. Serve pancakes as desired and enjoy!

Per Serving
calories: 171 | fat: 6g | protein: 14g | carbs: 14g | fiber: 0g | sugar: 1g | sodium: 305mg

Huevos Rancheros

Prep time: 5 minutes | Cook time: 15 to 20 minutes | Serves 2

1 (14-ounce / 397-g) can diced tomatoes with green chilies
1 teaspoon chili powder, plus more if desired
½ teaspoon onion powder
½ teaspoon garlic powder
4 eggs
Salt and freshly ground black pepper, to taste

1. For the sauce, mix undrained tomatoes, chili powder, onion powder and garlic powder in a medium nonstick skillet over medium heat and season to taste with salt and pepper. Heat tomato mixture to a boil, reduce heat, cover and simmer for about 5 minutes. 2. Make 4 wells in the tomato mixture. Crack an egg into a small bowl and pour into one of the wells. Repeat with remaining eggs. Sprinkle more chili powder over eggs if desired. 3. Cover skillet and simmer until eggs are cooked to desired consistency; about 5 minutes for soft and runny yolks, up to 10 minutes for firm and hard yolks. 4. Scoop eggs onto plates and top with the sauce to serve. Enjoy!

Per Serving

calories: 164 | fat: 9g | protein: 13g | carbs: 10g | fiber: 1g | sugar: 0g | sodium: 660mg

Taco Omelet

Prep time: 5 minutes | Cook time: 10 minutes | Serves 1

2 eggs, lightly beaten
2 tablespoons skim milk
¼ teaspoon chili powder
¼ teaspoon garlic powder
¼ teaspoon onion powder
Salt and freshly ground black pepper, to taste
1 teaspoon vegetable oil
1 tablespoon guacamole
1 tablespoon sour cream
1 tablespoon salsa
2 tablespoons shredded cheese

1. In a medium bowl, whisk eggs, milk, chili powder, garlic powder and onion powder and season to taste with salt and pepper. 2. Heat oil in a medium nonstick skillet over medium heat. Pour egg mixture into skillet and swirl to coat evenly. Cover skillet and let eggs cook until set on top, about 4 minutes. 3. With a large spatula, carefully flip omelet. Season omelet to taste with salt and pepper and let cook until lightly browned on the bottom, about 3 minutes more. 4. Slide omelet onto a plate. Spread guacamole, sour cream and salsa all over one side of the omelet and sprinkle with cheese. Fold omelet in half over filling and serve immediately. Enjoy

Per Serving

calories: 290 | fat: 22g | protein: 17g | carbs: 6g | fiber: 1g | sugar: 3g | sodium: 639mg

Apple Cinnamon Oatmeal

Prep time: 10 minutes | Cook time: 10 minutes | Serves 1

½ cup skim milk
⅓ cup water
1 apple, peeled, cored, diced
Dash of salt
½ cup old fashioned oats
¼ teaspoon cinnamon
¼ teaspoon vanilla

1. Mix milk, water, apple and salt in a small saucepan and heat to a simmer, stirring occasionally (do not boil). 2. Add oats and cinnamon to saucepan and simmer, uncovered, for about 5 minutes, stirring occasionally. 3. Stir vanilla into oatmeal and serve immediately. Enjoy!

Per Serving

calories: 446 | fat: 6g | protein: 18g | carbs: 84g | fiber: 13g | sugar: 25g | sodium: 228mg

Nutty Crunch Porridge

Prep time: 5 minutes | Cook time: 10 minutes | Serves 1

1 cup almond milk
3 tablespoons farina breakfast porridge mix (such as Cream of Wheat or Malt-O-Meal)
Dash of salt
1 tablespoons sliced almonds, toasted

1. In a small saucepan, heat almond milk to a simmer (do not boil). 2. Whisk farina into milk until smooth. 3. Reduce heat and simmer, uncovered, until porridge is thickened, about 2 minutes, stirring occasionally. 4. Stir salt into porridge. Pour porridge into a bowl and sprinkle with almonds to serve. Enjoy!

Per Serving

calories: 155 | fat: 11g | protein: 5g | carbs: 10g | fiber: 3g | sugar: 1g | sodium: 261mg

Make-Ahead Breakfast Burritos

Prep time: 15 minutes | Cook time: 20 minutes | Makes 8 burritos

12 large eggs
¼ cup low-fat milk
1 teaspoon extra-virgin olive oil
½ medium yellow onion, diced
1 medium green bell pepper, seeded and diced
1 cup canned black beans, drained and rinsed
8 (7- to 8-inch) whole wheat tortillas
½ cup shredded Cheddar cheese
8 ounces (227 g) salsa

1. In a large bowl, whisk together the eggs and milk. 2. In a large skillet over medium heat, heat the oil. Add the onion, bell pepper, and black beans. Sauté until the onion is translucent, about 5 minutes, and transfer to a plate. 3. Pour the egg mixture into the skillet, and gently stir until the eggs are fluffy and firm. Remove from the heat. 4. Divide the eggs and onion mixture evenly among the tortillas, and top with the cheese and salsa. 5. With both sides of the first tortilla tucked in, roll tightly to close. Repeat with the remaining tortillas. 6. Serve immediately, or freeze for up to 3 months. If freezing, wrap the burritos in paper towels, and cover tightly with aluminum foil for storage.

Per Serving

calories: 264 | fat: 12g | protein: 21g | carbs: 24g | fiber: 12g | sugar: 3g | sodium: 593mg

Pumpkin Spice Muffins

Prep time: 10 minutes | Cook time: 25 minutes | Makes 12 muffins

1½ cups whole wheat flour
2 teaspoons pumpkin pie spice
1 teaspoon baking soda
½ teaspoon salt
4 tablespoons butter, softened
⅔ cup erythritol
2 tablespoons maple syrup
1 teaspoon vanilla extract
2 large eggs

1. Preheat the oven to 350°F (180°C). Line a muffin tin with muffin liners. 2. In a large bowl, mix the flour, pumpkin pie spice, baking soda, and salt. 3. In another large bowl, using a hand mixer, mix the butter, erythritol, maple syrup, and vanilla until smooth. Add 1 egg at a time, beating until mixed. 4. Add the dry flour mixture to the wet ingredients in small amounts, mixing between each addition. 5. Divide the batter evenly among the 12 muffin cups. Bake for about 25 minutes, or until a toothpick inserted into the center comes out clean. Cool completely on a wire rack, then store in a resealable bag or air-tight container.

Per Serving

calories: 107 | fat: 5g | protein: 3g | carbs: 13g | fiber: 2g | sugar: 2g | sodium: 241mg

Smoked Salmon Breakfast Toast

Prep time: 10 minutes | Cook time: 0 minutes | Serves 4

2 tablespoons low-fat plain Greek yogurt
Juice of ½ lemon
1 very ripe avocado
4 slices sprouted-grain bread (100 percent whole-grain)
8 ounces (227 g) smoked salmon
2 fresh dill sprigs

1. In a small bowl, mix together the yogurt and lemon juice. 2. Cut open the avocado, remove the pit, and scoop out the flesh into the bowl with the yogurt. Mix well. The avocado mixture should be relatively smooth, without any large chunks. 2. Toast the bread. 3. Layer each toast slice with the avocado mixture and 2 ounces (57 g) of the smoked salmon, and top each with fresh dill. Serve immediately.

Per Serving (1 toast)
calories: 231 | fat: 10g | protein: 18g | carbs: 19g | fiber: 6g | sugar: 2g | sodium: 546mg

Smoothie Bowl with Greek Yogurt and Fresh Berries

Prep time: 5 minutes | Cook time: 5 minutes | Serves 1

¾ cup unsweetened vanilla almond milk or low-fat milk
¼ cup low-fat plain Greek yogurt
⅓ cup (1 handful) fresh spinach
½ scoop (⅛ cup) plain or vanilla protein powder
¼ cup frozen mixed berries
¼ cup fresh raspberries
¼ cup fresh blueberries
1 tablespoon sliced, slivered almonds
1 teaspoon chia seeds

1. In a blender, combine the milk, yogurt, spinach, protein powder, and frozen berries. Blend on high speed for 3 to 4 minutes, until the powder is well dissolved and no longer visible. 2. Pour the smoothie into small bowl. 3. Decorate the smoothie with the fresh raspberries, blueberries, almonds, and chia seeds. 4. Serve with a spoon and enjoy!

Per Serving (1 bowl)
calories: 255 | fat: 10g | protein: 20g | carbs: 21g | fiber: 8g | sugar: 10g | sodium: 262mg

Southwestern Scrambled Egg Burritos

Prep time: 10 minutes | Cook time: 10 minutes | Makes 8 burritos

12 eggs
¼ cup low-fat milk
1 teaspoon extra-virgin olive oil
½ onion, chopped
1 red bell pepper, diced
1 green bell pepper, diced
1 (15-ounce / 425-g) can black beans, drained and rinsed
8 (7- to 8-inch) whole-wheat tortillas, such as La Tortilla Factory low-carb tortillas
1 cup salsa, for serving

1. In a large bowl, whisk together the eggs and milk. Set aside. 2. In a large skillet over medium-high heat, heat the olive oil and add the onion and bell peppers. Sauté for 2 to 3 minutes, or until tender. Add the beans and stir to combine. 3. Add the egg mixture. Reduce the heat to medium-low and stir gently and constantly with a rubber spatula for 5 minutes, until the eggs are fluffy and cooked through. 4. Divide the scrambled egg mixture among the tortillas. Fold over the bottom end of the tortilla, fold in the sides, and roll tightly to close. 5. Serve immediately with the salsa, or place each burrito in a zip-top bag and refrigerate for up to 1 week. To eat, reheat each burrito in the microwave for 60 to 90 seconds. These will also keep well in the freezer for up to 1 month.

Per Serving (1 burrito)
calories: 250 | fat: 10g | protein: 19g | carbs: 28g | fiber: 13g | sugar: 1g | sodium: 546mg

Breakfast Almond Freezer Pops

Prep time: 10 minutes | Cook time: 0 minutes | Serves 8

2 cups plain unsweetened Greek yogurt
1 cup almond milk
2 ripe bananas, mashed
¼ cup almond butter
1 cup chopped strawberries

1. Whisk yogurt, milk and bananas until smooth. Add strawberries and almonds and stir until combined. 2. Spoon yogurt mixture into 6 freezer pop molds, set handled lids in place and freeze until firm, about 4 hours. Pops will keep in the freezer for about 2 weeks. Serve as desired and enjoy!

Per Serving
calories: 133 | fat: 9g | protein: 4g | carbs: 11g | fiber: 2g | sugar: 7g | sodium: 75mg

Clementine, Cranberry, and Pecan Bircher Muesli

Prep time: 10 minutes | Cook time: 0 minutes | Serves 4

1⅔ cups old-fashioned rolled oats
1 apple, cored and grated
⅔ cup low-fat milk
2 teaspoons pumpkin seeds
½ cup orange juice
2 ounces (57 g) dried cranberries
½ teaspoon ground cinnamon
1½ teaspoons maple or sugar-free fruit syrup
¾ cup fat-free plain Greek yogurt
1 clementine, peeled and segmented
8 toasted pecans

1. In a bowl, mix the oats with the apple, milk, pumpkin seeds, orange juice, half the cranberries, cinnamon, syrup, and yogurt, mixing well. Cover and leave to soak for at least 3 hours or ideally overnight in the refrigerator. 2. When ready to serve, spoon the muesli into bowls and top with the clementine segments and pecans. Scatter the remaining cranberries on top to serve.

Per Serving
calories: 243 | fat: 8g | protein: 12g | carbs: 48g | fiber: 9g | sugar: 18g | sodium: 57mg

Granola and Fruit Breakfast Tartlets

Prep time: 10 minutes | Cook time: 10 minutes | Serves 4

1½ cups low-sugar granola mix, or rolled oats
¼ cup mixed chopped nuts
2 tablespoons mixed seeds
1 tablespoon dried or flaked coconut
1 tablespoon coconut or other oil
2 tablespoons sugar-free syrup, agave syrup, or honey
1¼ cups fat-free Greek yogurt
2 teaspoons sweetener (optional)
Handful of berries, or about 6 ounces (170 g) prepared fresh fruit
Mint sprigs, to decorate

1. Preheat the oven to 350°F (180°C). Lightly grease 4 mini loose-bottomed tartlet pans. 2. Place the granola or oats, nuts, seeds, coconut, and coconut oil in a food processor and pulse to form a crumb-like consistency. Melt the coconut oil, if necessary (in the microwave for just a few seconds), then mix with the syrup, agave, or honey. Add to the granola mixture and pulse again to combine. Remove and divide among the tartlet pans. Make a crust for the tartlets by firmly pressing down on the bottom and sides of the pans so that you form a smooth base. Place on a baking sheet. Bake for 8 to 10 minutes or until the crust begins to brown—take care not to overcook, since the mixture burns easily. Remove from the oven and let cool in their pans. 3. To serve, remove the tartlets from their pans and place on a serving plate. Mix the yogurt with the sweetener, if using. Divide among the granola crusts and top with fruit to serve, garnished with mint sprigs.

Per Serving
calories: 307 | fat: 15g | protein: 12g | carbs: 47g | fiber: 8g | sugar: 20g | sodium: 66mg

Veggie and Egg Breakfast Sizzle

Prep time: 10 minutes | Cook time: 10 minutes | Serves 4

Low-fat cooking spray
1 small onion, chopped
3 zucchini, chopped
5 ounces (142 g) mushrooms, sliced

1 red bell pepper, cored, seeded, and chopped
2 tablespoons chopped fresh basil
Salt and freshly ground black pepper
4 large eggs

1. Generously spray a large nonstick frying pan with low-fat cooking spray. Heat, add the onion, zucchini, mushrooms, and bell pepper, and cook over a high heat for 4 to 6 minutes, stirring until golden and softened. Stir in the basil and salt and pepper. 2. Make 4 hollows in the mixture, then crack an egg into each. Reduce the heat, cover the pan, and cook for about 3 minutes, until the eggs are cooked and set to your liking. 3. Serve immediately with a little toast, if tolerated.

Per Serving
calories: 116 | fat: 5g | protein: 10g | carbs: 9g | fiber: 2g | sugar: 6g | sodium: 86mg

Breakfast Scones

Prep time: 10 minutes | Cook time: 20 minutes | Makes 10 scones

Low-fat cooking spray
1 cup mushrooms, chopped
1¼ cups all-purpose flour
1¼ teaspoons baking powder
¼ cup light butter or low-fat spread

5 ounces (142 g) lean bacon or turkey bacon, grilled or broiled and chopped
½ cup grated reduced-fat hard cheese
½ cup low-fat milk
Low-fat soft cheese, ham, and sliced tomatoes, to fill, as desired

1. Preheat the oven to 425ºF (220ºC). Grease a baking sheet with low-fat cooking spray. 2. Generously spray a small pan with low-fat cooking spray. Heat, add the mushrooms, and cook for 4 to 5 minutes, until golden. Let cool. 3. Mix the flour with baking powder in a large bowl. Rub in the butter or spread until the mixture resembles fine bread crumbs. 4. Stir in the bacon, mushrooms, and half of the cheese. Mix in the milk to form a soft dough. 5. Roll out the dough on a lightly floured surface to ¾-inch thickness. Stamp out rounds with a 2½-inch round cutter. The mixture will make about 10 scones. 6. Place on the baking sheet and sprinkle with the remaining cheese. 7. Bake for 10 to 15 minutes, until cooked and golden. 8. Serve warm or cold, filled with low-fat cheese, ham, and sliced tomatoes, if desired.

Per Serving
calories: 115 | fat: 3g | protein: 8g | carbs: 13g | fiber: 1g | sugar: 1g | sodium: 138mg

Protein Loaf

Prep time: 15 minutes | Cook time: 40 minutes | Makes 1 large loaf

2 cups ground almonds or almond flour
¼ cup plus 2 tablespoons coconut flour
1½ teaspoons baking powder
Scant ½ teaspoon baking soda
Large pinch of salt

7 large eggs
3 tablespoons melted butter or coconut oil
1 heaping tablespoon honey
1½ tablespoons apple cider vinegar
Golden flaxseeds or chopped nuts, to sprinkle (optional)

1. Preheat the oven to 375ºF (190ºC). Grease a large loaf pan (about 8½ inches long). 2. Mix the ground almonds with the coconut flour, baking powder, baking soda, and salt in a bowl. 3. In a second bowl, beat the eggs with the butter, honey, and vinegar. 4. Pour the egg mixture over the dry ingredients and whisk until smooth and combined. 5. Transfer to the loaf pan, smooth the top and sprinkle with the flaxseeds, if using. Bake for 35 to 40 minutes, until golden and shrinking from the sides of the pan. 6. Run a knife around the edges of the pan and turn out onto a wire rack to cool. Serve sliced.

Per Serving
calories: 152 | fat: 12g | protein: 7g | carbs: 3g | fiber: 0g | sugar: 2g | sodium: 214mg

Savory Stuffed Crepes

Prep time: 10 minutes | Cook time: 15 minutes | Serves 4

2 tablespoons butter, divided
2 scallions, sliced
1 garlic clove, minced
1 (3-ounce / 85-g) package cream cheese, softened
1 tablespoon sour cream

4 eggs
½ cup skim milk
¼ cup flour
Salt and freshly ground black pepper, to taste

Make the Filling: 1. Heat 1 tablespoon butter in a small nonstick skillet and sauté scallions until softened, about 2 minutes, stirring occasionally. Add garlic and sauté about 1 minute more, stirring constantly. Mix cream cheese and sour cream until smooth, add scallion mixture and stir until combined. Set filling aside. Make the Crepes: 2. Whisk eggs, milk and flour in a medium bowl and season to taste with salt and pepper. Melt remaining 1 tablespoon butter in a medium nonstick skillet over medium heat and fry portions of egg mixture into 4 crepes. 3. Spread about ¼ of the filling up the center of each crepe and roll up crepes to cover filling. Serve immediately and enjoy!

Per Serving
calories: 238 | fat: 18g | protein: 9g | carbs: 9g | fiber: 0g | sugar: 2g | sodium: 161mg

Chicken Livers and Scrambled Eggs

Prep time: 5 minutes | Cook time: 15 minutes | Serves 4

Butter-flavored cooking spray
1 large sweet onion, quartered and sliced
8 ounces (227 g) fresh mushrooms, sliced
1 pound (454 g) chicken livers, rinsed

4 large eggs, or 1 cup egg substitute lightly beaten with 1 teaspoon water
¼ teaspoon curry powder
Salt and pepper, to taste

1. Spray a large skillet with cooking spray and heat over medium heat until it shimmers. 2. Add onion and mushrooms, cooking until onion softens and mushrooms give up their liquid, 4 to 6 minutes. 3. While onions and mushrooms are cooking, trim connective tissue and roughly chop chicken livers. 4. Stir chicken livers into skillet and cook until they just start to brown, 5 to 7 minutes. 5. Mix eggs with curry powder and pour into skillet, stirring to coat livers, onion, and mushrooms. Cook, stirring constantly, for 1 to 2 minutes, or until eggs form small curds that are soft but not runny.

Per Serving
calories: 161 | fat: 11g | protein: 28g | carbs: 9g | fiber: 1g | sugar: 5g | sodium: 161mg

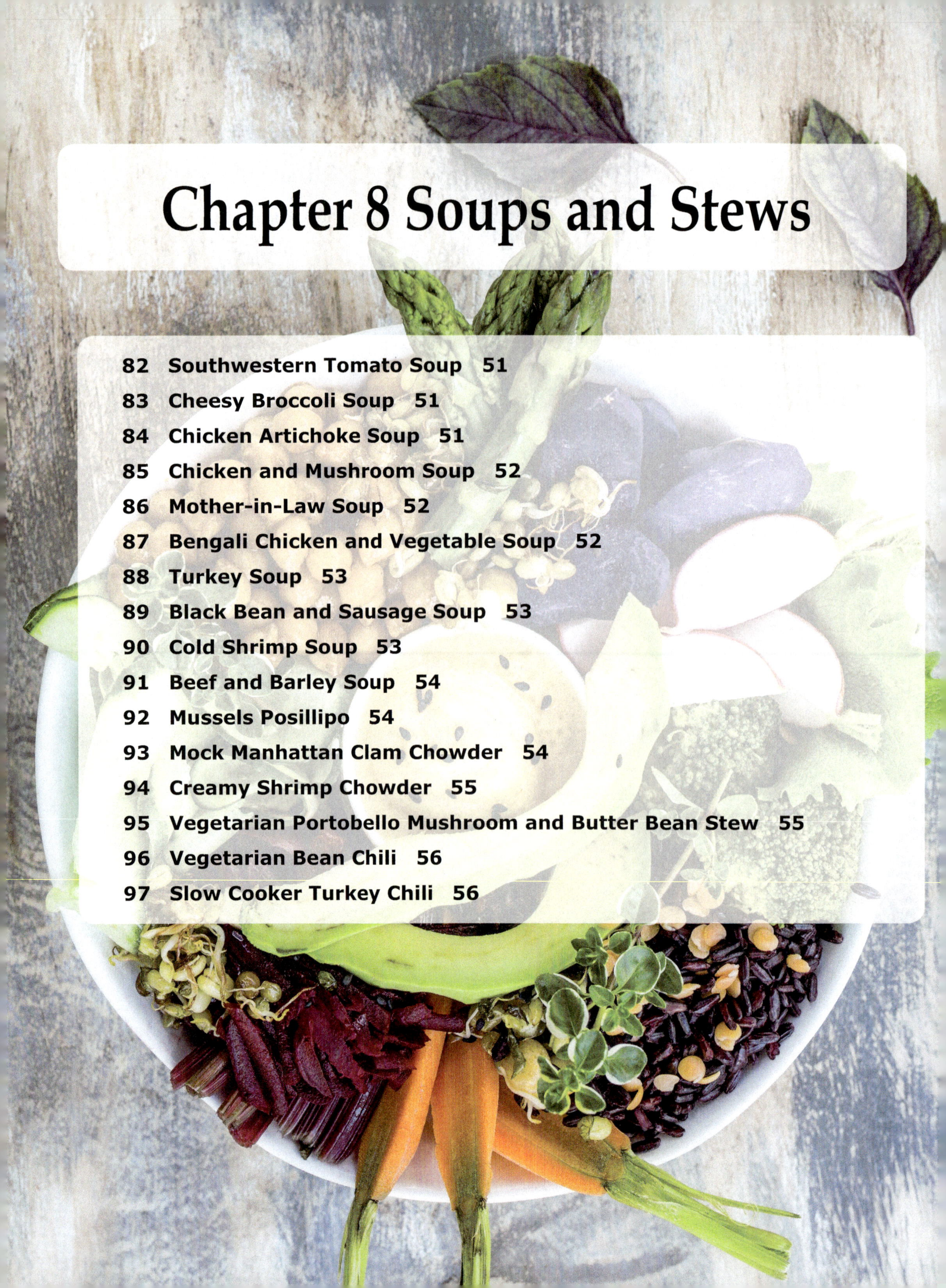

Chapter 8 Soups and Stews

82　**Southwestern Tomato Soup**　51
83　**Cheesy Broccoli Soup**　51
84　**Chicken Artichoke Soup**　51
85　**Chicken and Mushroom Soup**　52
86　**Mother-in-Law Soup**　52
87　**Bengali Chicken and Vegetable Soup**　52
88　**Turkey Soup**　53
89　**Black Bean and Sausage Soup**　53
90　**Cold Shrimp Soup**　53
91　**Beef and Barley Soup**　54
92　**Mussels Posillipo**　54
93　**Mock Manhattan Clam Chowder**　54
94　**Creamy Shrimp Chowder**　55
95　**Vegetarian Portobello Mushroom and Butter Bean Stew**　55
96　**Vegetarian Bean Chili**　56
97　**Slow Cooker Turkey Chili**　56

Southwestern Tomato Soup

Prep time: 10 minutes | Cook time: 48 minutes | Serves 4

Olive oil cooking spray
½ cup finely chopped onion
2 tablespoons minced garlic
½ teaspoon chili powder
½ teaspoon ground cumin
½ teaspoon dried oregano
1 bay leaf
1 (14½-ounce / 411-g) can diced tomatoes with liquid
1 (14½-ounce / 411-g) can fat-free, low-sodium chicken broth
½ pound (227 g) boneless, skinless turkey thighs (or any dark-meat turkey), cut up
Salt and pepper, to taste

1. Coat bottom of a large soup pot with cooking spray. Over medium heat, sauté onion and garlic for 3 minutes. 2. Stir in chili powder, cumin, oregano, and bay leaf. Add tomatoes, chicken broth, and turkey, and bring to a boil. 3. Lower heat, cover, and simmer for 45 minutes. Remove bay leaf. 4. Purée in batches in a blender or food processor. Or you can use an immersion blender and purée right in soup pot. Add salt and pepper to taste.

Per Serving
calories: 139 | fat: 6g | protein: 15g | carbs: 8g | fiber: 3g | sugar: 4g | sodium: 225mg

Cheesy Broccoli Soup

Prep time: 15 minutes | Cook time: 20 minutes | Serves 4

2 teaspoons butter
1 tablespoon minced onion
1 garlic clove, minced
3 cups chicken stock
4 cups broccoli florets
Salt and freshly ground black pepper, to taste
2 cups skim milk
½ cup shredded Colby cheese

1. In a large saucepan, melt butter and sauté onion until softened, about 5 minutes, stirring frequently. Add garlic and sauté about 1 minute more, stirring constantly. Add chicken stock and broccoli to pan, season to taste with salt and pepper and heat to a boil. Cover pan, reduce heat and simmer until broccoli is softened, 10 to 15 minutes, stirring occasionally. 2. Add milk to soup and stir until heated through, 1 to 2 minutes. 3. Remove pan from heat, add cheese and stir until cheese is melted. Serve soup immediately and enjoy!

Per Serving
calories: 176 | fat: 9g | protein: 14g | carbs: 13g | fiber: 0g | sugar: 6g | sodium: 238mg

Chicken Artichoke Soup

Prep time: 10 minutes | Cook time: 10 minutes | Serves 4

1 (14-ounce / 397-g) can artichoke hearts in brine, drained well
2 ounces (57 g) soft or silken tofu
3 tablespoons grated Parmesan cheese
1½ tablespoons fresh lemon juice
¾ teaspoon dried tarragon
2 teaspoons grated lemon zest
2 garlic cloves, minced
¼ teaspoon ground nutmeg
¼ teaspoon chili powder
2 cups fat-free, low-sodium chicken broth
½ pound (227 g) cooked skinless, boneless chicken breast, cubed

1. Purée artichoke hearts in food processor until chunky. 2. Add all remaining ingredients and purée until smooth. 3. Pour into large pot, cover, and simmer over low heat for 10 minutes.

Per Serving
calories: 164 | fat: 4g | protein: 21g | carbs: 14g | fiber: 6g | sugar: 1g | sodium: 229mg

Chicken and Mushroom Soup

Prep time: 10 minutes | Cook time: 40 minutes | Serves 4

Butter-flavored cooking spray
1½ cups chopped onion
3 garlic cloves, minced
1 pound (454 g) fresh white mushrooms, chopped
½ teaspoon dried tarragon
1 bay leaf
¼ teaspoon dried thyme
½ cup white wine
½ pound (227 g) boneless, skinless chicken breast, quartered
2 (14½-ounce / 411-g) cans fat-free, low-sodium chicken broth
⅓ cup dried shiitake mushrooms (about ½ ounce / 14 g)
¼ cup fat-free sour cream
Salt and pepper, to taste
2 tablespoons chopped fresh chives, or 1 tablespoon dried

1. Coat bottom of a large soup pot with cooking spray and sauté onion, garlic, and fresh mushrooms over medium heat. Cover and cook for 10 minutes, stirring occasionally. 2. Add tarragon, bay leaf, thyme, and wine, stirring and scraping bottom of pot to loosen browned bits. 3. Lower heat and add chicken, chicken broth, and dried mushrooms. Cover and simmer for 30 minutes. 4. Discard bay leaf and stir in sour cream. 5. Purée soup in batches in a food processor until smooth. Add salt and pepper to taste, and top with chives.

Per Serving

calories: 170 | fat: 3g | protein: 22g | carbs: 15g | fiber: 2g | sugar: 5g | sodium: 485mg

Mother-in-Law Soup

Prep time: 10 minutes | Cook time: 25 minutes | Serves 4

Olive oil cooking spray
4 large garlic cloves, minced
1 ounce (28 g) prosciutto, diced
1 teaspoon sweet paprika
¼ teaspoon ground cumin
¼ teaspoon freshly ground black pepper
⅛ teaspoon saffron threads
2 (14½-ounce / 411-g) cans fat-free, low-sodium chicken broth
4 large eggs
Salt to taste

1. In a large nonstick saucepan, heat cooking spray over medium-high heat until hot but not smoking. Sauté garlic for 1 minute. Add prosciutto and paprika, and sauté for 30 more seconds. 2. Stir in cumin, pepper, and saffron, add broth, and bring to a boil. 3. Cover pan, lower heat, and simmer for 20 minutes. 4. One at a time, carefully break eggs into soup and simmer for 3 minutes until whites are set. Add salt to taste. Serve soup with one poached egg per serving.

Per Serving

calories: 119 | fat: 6g | protein: 12g | carbs: 4g | fiber: 0g | sugar: 1g | sodium: 225mg

Bengali Chicken and Vegetable Soup

Prep time: 10 minutes | Cook time: 20 minutes | Serves 4

1 (14-ounce / 397-g) can unsweetened light coconut milk
1 medium onion, chopped
1 garlic clove, minced
¼ teaspoon dried thyme
¼ cup fresh parsley
2 whole cloves
½ teaspoon ground cinnamon
1 tablespoon finely minced fresh ginger
1 small fresh jalapeño pepper, seeded and finely chopped
1 (14½-ounce / 411-g) can fat-free, low-sodium chicken broth
½ pound (227 g) skinless chicken breast, diced
½ pound (227 g) cauliflower florets
½ pound (227 g) broccoli florets
1 large carrot, sliced
Salt and pepper, to taste

1. In a large soup pot, combine coconut milk, onion, garlic, thyme, parsley, cloves, cinnamon, ginger, and jalapeño. Bring to a simmer over medium heat and let cook, uncovered, stirring occasionally, for 15 to 20 minutes, or until thickened. Remove whole cloves. 2. Stir in chicken broth, chicken, cauliflower, broccoli, and carrot. Cover pot and simmer over low heat for 1 hour. Add salt and pepper to taste.

Per Serving

calories: 241 | fat:13 g | protein: 20g | carbs: 15g | fiber: 3g | sugar: 4g | sodium: 218mg

Turkey Soup

Prep time: 20 minutes | Cook time: 30 minutes | Serves 6

1 tablespoon butter
1 pound (454 g) boneless skinless turkey thighs
6 cups chicken stock
½ teaspoon kosher salt, plus more to taste
¼ teaspoon freshly ground black pepper, plus more to taste
2 celery stalks, diced
2 carrots, peeled, diced
1 small onion, diced
1½ teaspoons dried Italian herb seasoning
2 dried bay leaves

1. Melt butter in a stock pot or large saucepan over medium heat and sauté turkey thighs until browned on all sides, about 5 minutes. 2. Add chicken stock, salt and pepper to pot and heat to a boil. Reduce heat, cover pot and simmer for about 10 minutes. 3. Add celery, carrots, onion, herb seasoning and bay leaves to pot, season to taste with salt and pepper and stir to combine. Cover pot and simmer until vegetables are tender, about 15 minutes more. 4. Remove bay leaves from soup and discard. Remove turkey thighs from soup, cut into bite-size pieces and stir back into soup. Serve soup immediately and enjoy!

Per Serving
calories: 151 | fat: 5g | protein: 21g | carbs: 6g | fiber: 1g | sugar: 2g | sodium: 379mg

Black Bean and Sausage Soup

Prep time: 15 minutes | Cook time: 20 minutes | Serves 4 to 8

2 (15-ounce / 425-g) cans low-sodium black beans, drained and rinsed
2½ cups low-sodium chicken, beef, or turkey broth
Olive oil cooking spray
2 cups diced onion
2 garlic cloves, minced
1 teaspoon chili powder
½ teaspoon ground cumin
¼ teaspoon freshly ground black pepper
¼–½ teaspoon hot sauce
1 (16-ounce / 454-g) package frozen chopped spinach or kale, thawed
8 ounces (227 g) turkey kielbasa, diced
½ cup reduced-fat sour cream (optional)

1. Pour 1 cup black beans and ½ cup broth into blender. Blend until smooth. 2. Spray a large pot or Dutch oven with cooking spray and heat over medium-high heat until shimmering. 3. Sauté onion and garlic until soft but not browned, about 5 minutes. 4. Add bean purée, whole beans, remaining broth, seasonings, hot sauce, and spinach and bring to a boil. Lower heat, cover, and simmer for 15 minutes, stirring occasionally. 5. Stir in kielbasa and cook, stirring, for 5 minutes. 6. Ladle into bowls or mugs and top with sour cream, if desired.

Per Serving
calories: 254 | fat: 5g | protein: 21g | carbs: 32g | fiber: 13g | sugar: 3g | sodium: 525mg

Cold Shrimp Soup

Prep time: 5 minutes | Cook time: 0 minutes | Serves 4

2 cups low-fat buttermilk
1½ teaspoons dry mustard
¼ packet artificial sweetener
½ pound (227 g) cooked shrimp, peeled and cleaned
1 small cucumber, peeled, seeded, and chopped (about ½ cup)
1 tablespoon minced fresh chives
Salt and pepper, to taste

1. In a food processor, combine all ingredients, except salt and pepper, and purée until smooth.
2. Chill for 1 hour in refrigerator before serving. Add salt and pepper to taste.

Per Serving
calories: 136 | fat: 3g | protein: 19g | carbs: 9g | fiber: 0g | sugar: 8g | sodium: 213mg

Beef and Barley Soup

Prep time: 15 minutes | Cook time: 40 minutes | Serves 8

2 teaspoons extra-virgin olive oil
1½ pounds (680 g) sirloin steak, cut into 1-inch pieces
1 medium onion, chopped
1 celery stalk, chopped
2 large carrots, chopped
1 medium parsnip, peeled and chopped
1 (6-ounce / 170-g) can tomato paste
1 tablespoon dried thyme
2 teaspoons Worcestershire sauce
2 teaspoons red wine vinegar
¾ cup quick-cook barley
2 cups beef broth
2 cups water
¼ cup chopped fresh flat-leaf parsley

1. In a large stockpot or Dutch oven over medium heat, heat the olive oil. Add the sirloin pieces, and brown them on all sides, about 5 minutes. Remove the beef from the pot and set aside. 2. Add the onion, celery, carrots, and parsnip to the pot. Cook until tender, about 5 minutes. 3. Mix in the tomato paste, thyme, Worcestershire sauce, and red wine vinegar. 4. Add the beef and barley to the pot, and stir until well coated. 5. Add the broth and water. 6. Bring the soup to a simmer, reduce the heat to low, and cover and cook for 30 minutes, or until the barley is soft and the beef is cooked thoroughly. 7. Serve with the fresh parsley sprinkled on top.

Per Serving (1 cup)
calories: 289 | fat: 13g | protein: 20g | carbs: 23g | fiber: 5g | sugar: 5g | sodium: 288mg

Mussels Posillipo

Prep time: 10 minutes | Cook time: 15 minutes | Serves 4

Olive oil cooking spray
6 large garlic cloves, minced
2 tablespoons tomato paste
1 (28-ounce / 794-g) can tomato purée
½ cup chopped fresh basil
2 teaspoons dried oregano
½ cup bottled clam juice
½ cup dry red wine
3 pounds (1.4 kg) mussels (about 60 mussels), cleaned and de-bearded
Salt and pepper, to taste

1. In a large nonstick Dutch oven or stockpot, heat cooking spray over medium heat until hot but not smoking. Sauté garlic until soft, add tomato paste, and cook, stirring, until tomato paste browns. 2. Stir in tomato purée, basil, and oregano, lower heat, and cook, covered, for about 5 minutes. 3. Add clam juice and wine and bring to a boil. Cook, uncovered, for 5 minutes. 4. Add mussels and cover pot. Cook for 5 to 7 minutes, or until mussels open. Add salt and pepper to taste.

Per Serving
calories: 318 | fat: 6g | protein: 33g | carbs: 34g | fiber: 5g | sugar: 12g | sodium: 652mg

Mock Manhattan Clam Chowder

Prep time: 5 minutes | Cook time: 10 minutes | Serves 4

Olive oil cooking spray
1 cup chopped onion
3 large garlic cloves, minced
1 (28-ounce / 794-g) can stewed tomatoes
½ pound (227 g) cooked chopped fresh clams
2 tablespoons fresh basil, or 2 teaspoons dried
⅛ teaspoon hot sauce (optional)
Salt and pepper, to taste

1. Coat bottom of large nonstick saucepan with cooking spray and cook onion and garlic over low heat, covered, for 5 minutes, or until just translucent. 2. Add tomatoes, clams, basil, and hot sauce (if using), cover pan, and simmer for 5 minutes, or until heated through. Add salt and pepper to taste.

Per Serving
calories: 79 | fat: 1g | protein: 3g | carbs: 18g | fiber: 5g | sugar: 9g | sodium: 60mg

Creamy Shrimp Chowder

Prep time: 10 minutes | Cook time: 40 minutes | Serves 4

Butter-flavored cooking spray
¼ cup chopped onion
1 teaspoon chopped garlic
1 ounce (28 g) low-fat ham, finely diced
¼ teaspoon lemon-pepper

1 (8-ounce / 227-g) bottle clam juice
1 cup evaporated fat-free milk
½ pound (227 g) large shrimp, shelled and deveined, quartered
Salt and pepper, to taste

1. Pour 2 cups water into a large saucepan. Place cauliflower in steamer insert, put into saucepan, cover, and steam over medium heat for 20 minutes, or until very soft. 2. Coat bottom of a large saucepan with cooking spray and cook onion and garlic over medium heat until soft, about 2 minutes. 3. Stir in ham and lemon-pepper, then add clam juice and evaporated milk. 4. Cook, stirring constantly, over medium heat until just barely boiling. Lower heat to low and simmer, stirring occasionally, for 10 minutes (it should be slightly thickened). 5. Purée ½ cauliflower and add to soup, stir well, and simmer for 5 minutes. 6. Coarsely chop remaining cauliflower and add to soup. 7. Stir in shrimp and cook for 30 seconds to 1 minute, or until all shrimp pieces turn pink.

Per Serving
calories: 107 | fat: 1g | protein: 12g | carbs: 12g | fiber: 1g | sugar: 6g | sodium: 547mg

Vegetarian Portobello Mushroom and Butter Bean Stew

Prep time: 15 minutes | Cook time: 2 hours | Serves 4

Olive oil cooking spray
1 large onion, sliced
4 large portobello mushroom caps, thickly sliced
3 garlic cloves, minced
2 (14½-ounce / 411-g) cans butter beans or lima beans, drained and rinsed

2 teaspoons dried thyme
1 teaspoon lemon-pepper
1 (28-ounce / 794-g) can low-sodium whole peeled tomatoes
1½ cups low-sodium vegetable broth
1 tablespoon Marmite or concentrated vegetarian broth

1. In a large pot, heat olive oil spray over medium-high heat until it shimmers. 2. Add onion, mushrooms, and garlic. Cover and cook until onion is translucent and mushrooms begin to give up their liquid, 7 to 10 minutes. 3. Stir in beans, thyme, and lemon-pepper. 4. Add tomatoes and smash them with back of a spoon. Stir in broth and Marmite or concentrate. 5. Cover and simmer over low heat for 2 hours, stirring occasionally, until thick and most of liquid has evaporated.

Per Serving
calories: 336 | fat: 1g | protein: 20g | carbs: 63g | fiber: 16g | sugar: 21g | sodium: 265mg

Vegetarian Bean Chili

Prep time: 20 minutes | Cook time: 2 hours | Serves 8 to 12

Olive oil cooking spray
1 medium carrot, peeled and diced
1 medium yellow onion, peeled and diced
2 garlic cloves, minced
1 medium red, yellow, or orange bell pepper, seeded and diced
1 jalapeño pepper, ribs and seeds removed, minced
3 celery stalks, diced
½ teaspoon dried oregano
1 teaspoon ground cumin
1 teaspoon chili powder
1 (15½-ounce / 439-g) can low-sodium diced tomatoes with chiles
1 (15½-ounce / 439-g) can low-sodium tomato sauce
1 cup low-sodium vegetable broth
1 (15½-ounce / 439-g) can low-sodium kidney beans, drained and rinsed
1 (15½-ounce / 439-g) can low-sodium pinto beans, drained and rinsed
1 (15½-ounce / 439-g) can low-sodium black beans, drained and rinsed
2 medium zucchini, diced
Salt, to taste

1. Coat a large lidded pot with cooking spray and heat over medium-high heat until hot. 2. Add carrot, onion, garlic, bell pepper, jalapeño, and celery and cook, stirring, for 7 to 9 minutes, or until onion turns golden brown. 3. Stir in oregano, cumin, and chili powder and cook for 2 minutes. 4. Pour in diced tomatoes, tomato sauce, and broth and bring to a boil, then lower heat to low and simmer, stirring, for 30 minutes. 5. Stir in beans and zucchini, cover pot, and simmer for 45 minutes to 1 hour, or until thick (if too soupy, increase heat and cook, uncovered, stirring, for 15 minutes more). 6. Add salt to taste.

Per Serving
calories: 204 | fat: 1g | protein: 14g | carbs: 33g | fiber: 13g | sugar: 8g | sodium: 577mg

Slow Cooker Turkey Chili

Prep time: 10 minutes | Cook time: 8 hours | Serves 16

Nonstick cooking spray
2 pounds (907 g) extra-lean ground turkey
2 (14½-ounce / 411-g) cans kidney beans, drained and rinsed
1 (28-ounce / 794-g) can diced tomatoes with green chiles
1 (8-ounce / 227-g) can tomato purée
1 large onion, finely chopped
1 green bell pepper, finely chopped
2 celery stalks, finely chopped
4 teaspoons minced garlic
1 teaspoon dried oregano
2 tablespoons ground cumin
3 tablespoons chili powder
1 (8-ounce / 227-g) can tomato juice

1. Place a large skillet over medium-high heat and coat it with the cooking spray. Add the ground turkey. Using a wooden spoon, break it into smaller pieces and cook until browned, 7 to 9 minutes. 2. While the turkey browns, place the beans, tomatoes, tomato purée, onion, bell pepper, celery, garlic, oregano, cumin, chili powder, and tomato juice in the slow cooker. Stir in the cooked ground turkey and mix well. 3. Cover the slow cooker and turn on low to cook for 8 hours. 4. Serve garnished with Greek yogurt, shredded Cheddar cheese, and chopped scallions (if using).

Per Serving (½ cup)
calories: 140 | fat: 4g | protein: 14g | carbs: 12g | fiber: 4g | sugar: 4g | sodium: 280mg

Chapter 9 Vegetables and Sides

- 98　Parmesan Spaghetti Squash　58
- 99　Mexican Cauliflower "Rice"　58
- 100　Saucy Garlic Broccoli　58
- 101　Zoodles with Pesto　59
- 102　Creamed Spinach　59
- 103　Kale with Apple and Onion　59
- 104　Marinated String Beans　60
- 105　Minted Cucumbers with Yogurt　60
- 106　Eggplant Rollatini　60
- 107　Dan's Crock Pickles　61
- 108　Roasted Carrots with Herbed Yogurt　61
- 109　Beet and Parsnip Fritters with Horseradish Yogurt Drizzle　61
- 110　Honey Roasted Brussels Sprouts　62
- 111　Roasted Root Vegetables　62
- 112　Quick and Simple Vegetable Stir-Fry　62
- 113　Peperonata　63
- 114　Ricotta, Celery, and Radish Baked Sweet Potato　63
- 115　Fresh Veggie Burgers　63

Parmesan Spaghetti Squash

Prep time: 15 minutes | Cook time: 45 to 50 minutes | Serves 4

1 large spaghetti squash
1 teaspoon olive oil
Salt and freshly ground black pepper, to taste
½ cup marinara sauce
1 teaspoon garlic powder
1 teaspoon garlic salt
½ cup finely grated Parmesan cheese

1. Preheat oven to 400ºF (205ºC). 2. Cut squash in half lengthwise and scoop out the seeds. Brush cut surfaces of squash with olive oil and season to taste with salt and pepper. 3. Place squash halves cut-sides down on a rimmed baking sheet and bake until tender, 45 to 50 minutes. 4. Scrape squash into strands from the peels with a fork. Toss squash strands with marinara sauce, garlic powder and onion powder and sprinkle with Parmesan cheese to serve. Enjoy!

Per Serving
calories: 188 | fat: 7g | protein: 6g | carbs: 29g | fiber: 6g | sugar: 11g | sodium: 294mg

Mexican Cauliflower "Rice"

Prep time: 20 minutes | Cook time: 5 minutes | Serves 4

1 teaspoon ground cumin
1 teaspoon chili powder
½ teaspoon paprika
½ teaspoon ancho chili powder
½ teaspoon garlic powder
½ teaspoon onion powder
1 medium head cauliflower, cored, cut into florets
1 tablespoon vegetable oil
1 tablespoon water, plus more if necessary
Salt, to taste
1 tablespoon guacamole

1. In a small bowl, mix cumin, chili powder, paprika, ancho chili powder, garlic powder and onion powder and set aside. 2. Pulse cauliflower florets in a food processor until grainy. Do not over-process or cauliflower will be too soft. 3. Heat oil in a medium nonstick skillet over medium heat and sauté cauliflower until tender and lightly golden, 4 to 5 minutes, stirring frequently. 4. Remove cauliflower from heat, sprinkle with water and stir to coat. Sprinkle spice mixture over cauliflower and season to taste with salt. Stir cauliflower to coat with spices, adding more water if necessary. 5. Spoon cauliflower into bowls, garnish with guacamole and serve immediately. Enjoy!

Per Serving
calories: 87 | fat: 5g | protein: 3g | carbs: 9g | fiber: 4g | sugar: 3g | sodium: 86mg

Saucy Garlic Broccoli

Prep time: 15 minutes | Cook time: 15 minutes | Serves 4

2 stalks broccoli, cut into bite-size pieces
Salt and freshly ground black pepper, to taste
1 tablespoon olive oil
2 garlic cloves, minced
1 tablespoon ginger, minced
2 cups chicken stock
2 tablespoons soy sauce
½ teaspoon red pepper flakes
2 tablespoons cornstarch
¼ cup chopped salted cashews

1. Pour water into a large saucepan to a depth of about 2 inches. Set steamer basket in saucepan, place broccoli in basket and season to taste with salt and pepper. Cover pan and steam over medium heat until broccoli is soft, 8 to 10 minutes. 2. Transfer broccoli to a serving dish, cover to keep warm and set aside. Empty cooking water from pan. 3. For the sauce, in the same pan, heat oil over medium heat and sauté garlic and ginger for about 1 minute. Add chicken broth, soy sauce and red pepper flakes to pan, season to taste with salt and pepper and heat to a simmer, stirring occasionally, about 10 minutes. 4. Dissolve cornstarch in about ¼ cup cold water, whisk into sauce and cook until sauce is thickened, stirring constantly, about 2 minutes. 5. Pour sauce over broccoli and stir gently to coat. Sprinkle cashews over broccoli and serve immediately. Enjoy!

Per Serving
calories: 206 | fat: 14g | protein: 7g | carbs: 16g | fiber: 1g | sugar: 3g | sodium: 220mg

Zoodles with Pesto

Prep time: 40 minutes | Cook time: 10 minutes | Serves 4

3 medium zucchini
1 teaspoon salt, plus more to taste
2 tablespoons pine nuts
½ cup fresh basil leaves, stems removed
1 garlic clove, minced
½ teaspoon lemon juice
2 tablespoons extra virgin olive oil
2 tablespoons grated Romano cheese
1 tablespoon vegetable oil

1. Cut zucchini into thin, noodle-like strips with a spiralizer, mandoline or vegetable peeler. Place zucchini in a colander, sprinkle with ½ teaspoon salt to draw out moisture and let stand while you prepare the pesto. 2. For the pesto, toast pine nuts in a medium dry nonstick skillet over medium heat until lightly browned, 2 to 3 minutes, stirring frequently. 3. Process toasted pine nuts, basil, garlic, lemon juice and ¼ teaspoon salt in a food processor and process until finely minced. 4. Continue processing pesto mixture, add olive oil in a slow thin stream and process until smooth. Add cheese and process just until combined. 5. Blot zoodles as dry as possible with paper towels. Heat vegetable oil in a medium nonstick skillet over medium heat and sauté zoodles until golden, 3 to 4 minutes, stirring frequently. Season zoodles with remaining ¼ teaspoon salt plus more to taste. 6. Spoon zoodles onto 4 plates, top with pesto and serve immediately. Enjoy!

Per Serving
calories: 121 | fat: 13g | protein: 1g | carbs: 1g | fiber: 0g | sugar: 0g | sodium: 582mg

Creamed Spinach

Prep time: 5 minutes | Cook time: 15 minutes | Serves 4

1 (10-ounce / 283-g) package frozen chopped spinach, thawed
Butter-flavored cooking spray
¼ cup thinly sliced shallots
⅓ cup skim milk
½ cup fat-free cream cheese
¼ teaspoon ground nutmeg (optional)
Salt and pepper, to taste

1. Place thawed spinach in two layers of paper towels and squeeze to remove as much liquid as possible. 2. Coat a saucepan with cooking spray and heat over medium heat until hot. 3. Add shallots and sauté until lightly browned. 4. Lower heat, add milk, cream cheese, and nutmeg (if using), and whisk until smooth. 5. Stir in spinach, cover pan, and simmer for 10 minutes. Remove lid, increase heat to medium, and cook for 1 minute more to thicken slightly. Add salt and pepper to taste.

Per Serving
calories: 69 | fat: 1g | protein: 9g | carbs: 8g | fiber: 2g | sugar: 4g | sodium: 314mg

Kale with Apple and Onion

Prep time: 5 minutes | Cook time: 10 minutes | Serves 4

1 medium Granny Smith apple, peeled and cored
Olive oil cooking spray
¾ cup chopped onion
⅛ teaspoon curry powder
1 bunch kale, tough stems and ribs removed, coarsely chopped (about 4 cups)
½ cup water

1. Cut apple into wedges, then into ¼-inch slices. 2. Coat a 4- to 5-quart nonstick pot with cooking spray and heat over medium-high heat until hot but not smoking. Sauté onion, stirring occasionally, until golden. 3. Stir in apple and curry powder, lower heat, cover pot, and cook for 2 minutes, or until apple is almost tender. 4. Add kale and water and cook, covered, for about 5 minutes, or until kale is tender and most of liquid has evaporated.

Per Serving
calories: 69 | fat: 1g | protein: 3g | carbs: 14g | fiber: 4g | sugar: 6g | sodium: 28mg

Marinated String Beans

Prep time: 10 minutes | Cook time: 9 minutes | Serves 4

½ pound (227 g) string beans, tips cut off
2 cups diced seeded tomato
5 garlic cloves, peeled and cut in half horizontally
1 tablespoon dried basil

¼ cup water
2 teaspoons olive oil
1 tablespoon balsamic vinegar
Salt and freshly ground pepper to taste

1. In a medium microwave-safe bowl, combine beans, tomato, garlic, basil, and water. 2. Cover and microwave on high for 9 minutes, or until beans are soft. 3. Let bean mixture cool and then toss with oil, vinegar, and salt and pepper to taste. 4. Serve it hot or cold (if you don't like a strong garlic flavor, remove garlic before serving).

Per Serving
calories: 84 | fat: 4g | protein: 3g | carbs: 11g | fiber: 3g | sugar: 4g | sodium: 189mg

Minted Cucumbers with Yogurt

Prep time: 5 minutes | Cook time: 0 minutes | Serves 4

2 large cucumbers, peeled and seeded (about 3 cups)
1 cup plain, fat-free yogurt
1 garlic clove, peeled and quartered

2 teaspoons fresh lemon juice
½ teaspoon ground cumin
2 teaspoons minced fresh mint leaves, or 1 teaspoon dried

1. Dice cucumbers. 2. Combine all ingredients, except cucumbers, in a food processor and process until smooth. 3. In a large bowl, toss cucumbers with yogurt mixture.

Per Serving
calories: 54 | fat: 0g | protein: 4g | carbs: 8g | fiber: 1g | sugar: 7g | sodium: 51mg

Eggplant Rollatini

Prep time: 15 minutes | Cook time: 50 minutes | Makes 6 to 8 rollatini

Nonstick cooking spray
1 large eggplant
1 tablespoon salt
1 teaspoon extra-virgin olive oil
1 pound (454 g) fresh spinach (about 10 cups)
½ cup part-skim ricotta cheese

¾ cup shredded part-skim Mozzarella cheese, divided
¼ cup shredded Parmigiano-Reggiano cheese
1 egg
1 teaspoon minced garlic
½ cup low-sugar jarred marinara sauce, divided

1. Preheat the oven to 400ºF (205ºC). Spray 1 or 2 baking sheets with the cooking spray. 2. Slice the eggplant lengthwise into ¼-inch pieces. Lay the slices on a paper towel and sprinkle them with salt. Let them sit for 10 minutes to help release some of the water in the eggplant. Pat dry afterward. It's okay to wipe off some of the salt before baking. 3. Place the eggplant on the baking sheet and bake for 10 minutes. Remove from the oven and set aside to cool. Leave the oven on. 4. Put a large pot over medium-high heat. Heat the olive oil for 1 minute. Add the spinach leaves and cook, stirring occasionally, for about 3 minutes or until wilted. Set aside to let cool. 5. Combine the ricotta, ¼ cup of Mozzarella, Parmigiano-Reggiano, egg, and garlic in a medium bowl. Mix well. When the spinach is cool, gently stir it into the cheese mixture. 6. Spread ¼ cup of the marinara sauce across the bottom of an 8-by-8-inch baking dish. 7. Spread the cheese mixture (about 2 tablespoons each) onto each eggplant slice, roll the slice, and place seam-side down in the baking dish. Continue until all eggplant slices are made into roll-ups and placed in the pan. 8. Top the rolled eggplant with the remaining ¼ cup of marinara and ½ cup of Mozzarella. 9. Reduce the oven temperature to 350ºF (180ºC). Cover the baking sheets with aluminum foil and bake for 30 minutes. Remove the foil and bake for an additional 10 minutes, or until the cheese is brown and bubbly.

Per Serving (2 rollatini)
calories: 160 | fat: 7g | protein: 11g | carbs: 16g | fiber: 6g | sugar: 8g | sodium: 330mg

Dan's Crock Pickles

Prep time: 10 minutes | Cook time: 5 minutes | Serves 10 to 15

6½ cups water
2 cups distilled white vinegar
¼ cup canning salt

4 fresh dill sprigs
3 garlic cloves
10 to 15 pickling cucumbers

1. In a large pot over high heat, bring the water, vinegar, and salt to a boil. When it reaches a rapid boil, turn off the stove and let the liquid sit to cool for 10 minutes. 2. Meanwhile, add the dill sprigs, garlic cloves, and pickling cucumbers to a gallon-size glass jar with an airtight lid. 3. Pour the brine mixture over the cucumbers; they should be completely covered by the liquid. Tightly seal the jar with its lid. 4. Let the pickles stand on the counter for 3 to 5 days. At this point the pickles are ready to eat or be refrigerated. They will keep for 2 months in the refrigerator.

Per Serving (1 pickle)

calories: 9 | fat: 0g | protein: 0g | carbs: 2g | fiber: 0g | sugar: 0g | sodium: 606mg

Roasted Carrots with Herbed Yogurt

Prep time: 5 minutes | Cook time: 25 minutes | Serves 4

1 pound (454 g) carrots, peeled
1 tablespoon extra-virgin olive oil, plus 2 teaspoons, divided
1 cup plain nonfat Greek yogurt
½ cup fresh mint leaves

½ cup fresh basil leaves
2 garlic cloves, peeled
Salt
Freshly ground black pepper

1. Preheat the oven to 400ºF (205ºC). 2. In a bowl, toss the carrots with 1 tablespoon olive oil and place on a baking sheet. Roast for about 25 minutes, until golden brown. 3. While the carrots roast, make the yogurt dip. In a blender or food processor, combine the yogurt, mint, basil, and garlic and process to combine. Add the remaining two teaspoons of oil to the yogurt dip and stir to combine. Season with salt and pepper. 4. Serve the carrots with the yogurt dip on the side.

Per Serving

calories: 136 | fat: 6g | protein: 7g | carbs: 14g | fiber: 4g | sugar: 8g | sodium: 109mg

Beet and Parsnip Fritters with Horseradish Yogurt Drizzle

Prep time: 10 minutes | Cook time: 20 minutes | Serves 4

Low-fat cooking spray
1 onion, chopped
2 garlic cloves, crushed
2 parsnips, peeled and coarsely grated
2 carrots, peeled and coarsely grated
2 beets, peeled and coarsely grated

2 eggs, beaten
1 small bunch fresh dill, chopped
2 teaspoons chopped fresh mint
Salt and freshly ground black pepper
1 cup fat-free plain or coconut yogurt
1½ teaspoons prepared horseradish

1. Generously spray a small skillet with low-fat cooking spray. Heat, add the onion and garlic, and cook until softened, about 5 minutes. Set aside. 2. Mix the parsnips with the carrot and beets, then squeeze with hands or in a paper towel to remove as much liquid as possible. 3. Add the eggs, half of the dill, the mint, the cooked onion and garlic, and salt and pepper, and mix well. 4. Generously spray a large frying pan with low-fat cooking spray. Heat over medium heat, then add heaping spoonfuls of the mixture to the pan to make patty shapes about 2½ inches in diameter. You will have to cook in 2 to 3 batches, and the mixture will make about 12 fritters. Cook for 3 to 4 minutes on each side, turning very gently with a spatula. It may be necessary to spray the pan again between batches. Keep warm. 5. Meanwhile, mix the remaining dill with the yogurt and horseradish. 6. Serve the fritters warm with the sauce drizzled over.

Per Serving

calories: 167 | fat: 3g | protein: 9g | carbs: 29g | fiber: 6g | sugar: 14g | sodium: 149mg

Honey Roasted Brussels Sprouts

Prep time: 5 minutes | Cook time: 25 minutes | Serves 4

2 tablespoons extra-virgin olive oil
2 tablespoons balsamic vinegar
1 tablespoon honey
3 cups Brussels sprouts, trimmed and halved
1 tablespoon white sesame seeds, for serving

1. Preheat the oven to 400ºF (205ºC). 2. In a bowl, combine the olive oil, balsamic vinegar, and honey and mix to incorporate. 3. Toss the Brussels sprouts with the oil mixture and spread in an even layer on a baking sheet. Roast for about 25 minutes, until well crisped and golden brown. 4. To serve, toss with the sesame seeds. Serve warm.

Per Serving
calories: 121 | fat: 8g | protein: 3g | carbs: 12g | fiber: 3g | sugar: 6g | sodium: 20mg

Roasted Root Vegetables

Prep time: 15 minutes | Cook time: 45 minutes | Makes about 6 cups

Nonstick cooking spray
2 medium red beets, peeled
2 large parsnips, peeled
2 large carrots, peeled
1 medium butternut squash (about 2 pounds / 907-g), peeled and seeded
1 medium red onion
2 tablespoons extra-virgin olive oil
4 teaspoons minced garlic
2 teaspoons dried thyme

1. Preheat the oven to 425ºF (220ºC). Spray a large rimmed baking sheet with the cooking spray. 2. Roughly chop the beets, parsnips, carrots, and butternut squash into 1-inch pieces. Cut the onion into half and then each half into 4 large chunks. 3. Arrange the vegetables in a single, even layer on the baking sheet, and sprinkle them with the olive oil, garlic, and thyme. Use a spoon to mix the vegetables to coat them with the oil and seasonings. 4. Roast for 45 minutes, stirring the vegetables every 15 minutes, until all the vegetables are tender. 5. Serve immediately.

Per Serving (½ cup)
calories: 68 | fat: 3g | protein: 1g | carbs: 11g | fiber: 1g | sugar: 5g | sodium: 30mg

Quick and Simple Vegetable Stir-Fry

Prep time: 10 minutes | Cook time: 5 minutes | Serves 4

2 teaspoons sesame oil, or low-fat cooking spray
2 garlic cloves, crushed
1 chile, finely chopped
1 onion, sliced
1 pound (454 g) mushrooms, sliced or halved
1 pound (454 g) Napa cabbage, coarsely chopped or shredded
11 ounces (312 g) canned baby corn, halved lengthwise
2 red bell peppers, cored, seeded, and sliced
¼ cup soy sauce
Small handful chopped cilantro (optional)

1. Place the oil in a large wok or pan, or generously spray the pan with low-fat cooking spray, then heat to hot. 2. Add the garlic and chile and cook for 30 seconds. 3. Add the onion, mushrooms, Napa cabbage, baby corn, and bell peppers, and stir-fry for about 4 minutes, or until tender-crisp. 4. Add the soy sauce, mixing and tossing well. 5. Spoon into serving bowls and sprinkle with the cilantro, if using, and serve.

Per Serving
calories: 125 | fat: 4g | protein: 9g | carbs: 14g | fiber: 4g | sugar: 6g | sodium: 214mg

Peperonata

Prep time: 10 minutes | Cook time: 25 minutes | Serves 4

Low-fat cooking spray
2 red onions, peeled and thinly sliced
2 garlic cloves, crushed
2 bay leaves
4 red bell peppers, seeded and thinly sliced
2 yellow bell peppers, seeded and thinly sliced
1 (14-ounce / 397-g) can diced tomatoes
Salt and freshly ground black pepper
2 tablespoons chopped fresh basil

1. Generously spray a large nonstick pan with low-fat cooking spray. Heat, add the onions, garlic, and bay leaves, and cook gently for 5 minutes, stirring occasionally. 2. Add the bell peppers, tomatoes, and salt and pepper, mixing well. Cook, uncovered, for about 20 minutes, stirring occasionally. Discard the bay leaves. 3. Stir in the basil and serve warm, or let cool and then chill until ready to serve.

Per Serving

calories: 120 | fat: 1g | protein: 4g | carbs: 23g | fiber: 6g | sugar: 14g | sodium: 208mg

Ricotta, Celery, and Radish Baked Sweet Potato

Prep time: 10 minutes | Cook time: 40 minutes | Serves 1

1 small sweet potato
Low-fat cooking spray
1 tablespoon ricotta
Salt and freshly ground black pepper
½ stalk celery, sliced
3 radishes, sliced
2 cherry tomatoes, quartered
1 teaspoon pumpkin or sunflower seeds, toasted, if desired

1. Preheat the oven to 400°F (205°C). Scrub the sweet potato, prick in a couple of places, and spray lightly with cooking spray. 2. Bake for 30 to 40 minutes (depending upon the size), until tender. Remove and allow to cool slightly. 3. Meanwhile, season the ricotta with salt and pepper to taste. 4. Make a deep slit lengthwise along the sweet potato, open it out, and carefully mash the potato flesh with a fork. Top with the ricotta, celery, radishes, tomatoes, and seeds to serve.

Per Serving

calories: 158 | fat: 3g | protein: 5g | carbs: 29g | fiber: 5g | sugar: 7g | sodium: 97mg
Fresh Veggie Burgers

Fresh Veggie Burgers

Prep time: 10 minutes | Cook time: 15 minutes | Serves 4

1 (15-ounce / 425-g) can low-sodium pinto beans, drained and rinsed
Cooking spray
1 small white or yellow onion, diced small
1 garlic clove, minced
3 green onions or scallions, thinly sliced
1 teaspoon cumin
¾ cup diced fresh mushrooms
1 teaspoon dried parsley
Salt and pepper, to taste

1. In a bowl, mash pinto beans with a fork or potato masher until smooth. Or pulse in a food processor until smooth. 2. Spray a skillet with cooking spray. Heat over medium heat until it shimmers. 3. Sauté onion and garlic for 3 to 5 minutes, or until soft. 4. Add green onions, cumin, mushrooms, and parsley and cook, stirring occasionally, for 5 minutes. Remove from pan. 5. Mix mashed beans with mushroom mixture and salt and pepper to taste, and form into 1-inch-thick patties. 6. Wipe out skillet, re-spray, and sauté patties for 3 to 4 minutes on each side, or until cooked through.

Per Serving

calories: 122 | fat: 0g | protein: 8g | carbs: 21g | fiber: 8g | sugar: 9g | sodium: 120mg

Chapter 10 Poultry

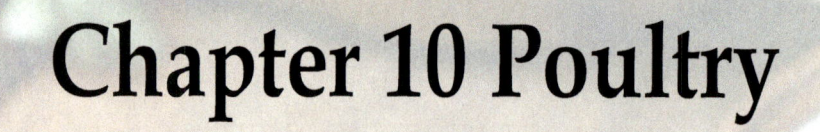

116 Chicken Cauliflower Bowls   65
117 Pulled Chicken   65
118 Lemon Chicken   65
119 Chicken Curry Wraps   66
120 Chicken Caprese   66
121 Creamy Pepper Chicken Skillet   66
122 DZ's Grilled Chicken Wings   67
123 Almond-Crusted Chicken Tenders   67
124 Chicken Breasts Stuffed with Ham and Cheese   67
125 Baked Garlic–Greek Yogurt Chicken with Parmesan   68
126 One-Pan Chicken and Broccoli   68
127 Chicken Burgers with Scallions and Ginger   68
128 Skillet Sausage with Peppers and Onions   69
129 Turkey Cutlets Francese   69
130 Turkey Cacciatore   69
131 Turkey Curry   70
132 Baked Turkey Meatballs   70

Chicken Cauliflower Bowls

Prep time: 20 minutes | Cook time: 12 minutes | Serves 4

1 large head cauliflower, cored
½ cup chicken stock, plus more if needed
1 teaspoon butter
¼ cup chopped onion

¼ cup chopped bell pepper
1 cup chopped cooked chicken breast
1 teaspoon garlic powder
Salt and freshly ground black pepper, to taste
¼ cup shredded white Cheddar cheese

1. Pour water into a large saucepan to a depth of about 2 inches. Set steamer basket in saucepan and place cauliflower in basket. Cover pan and steam over medium heat until cauliflower is soft, 10 to 12 minutes. 2. Meanwhile, heat butter in a medium nonstick skillet and sauté onion and bell pepper until softened, 4 to 5 minutes, stirring frequently. Remove skillet from heat, add cooked chicken and garlic powder, season to taste with salt and pepper and stir to combine. 3. Carefully remove cauliflower from steamer basket and place in a large bowl. Crumble and lightly mash cauliflower with a fork and season to taste with salt and pepper. Add chicken stock to cauliflower and purée with an immersion blender until smooth, adding more stock if needed. 4. Scoop cauliflower into 4 bowls, top with the chicken mixture and sprinkle with the grated cheese to serve. Enjoy!

Per Serving

calories: 159 | fat: 6g | protein: 17g | carbs: 12g | fiber: 4g | sugar: 5g | sodium: 148mg

Pulled Chicken

Prep time: 15 minutes | Cook time: 8 to 10 hours | Serves 3

1 small onion, cut into strips
1 small bell pepper, cut into strips
1 garlic clove, minced

1 tablespoon taco seasoning or barbecue spice rub, plus more if desired
2 boneless skinless chicken breasts

1. Arrange onion and bell pepper strips in the bottom of a 3- to 4-quart slow cooker and sprinkle with garlic. 2. Rub chicken breasts all over with taco seasoning and place in slow cooker. 3. Cover slow cooker and cook chicken on low until cooked through and tender, 8 to 10 hours. 4. Remove chicken from slow cooker and shred with two forks. Add juices from slow cooker to chicken and sprinkle with additional taco seasoning if desired. Serve immediately and enjoy!

Per Serving

calories: 142 | fat: 3g | protein: 24g | carbs: 7g | fiber: 1g | sugar: 4g | sodium: 386mg

Lemon Chicken

Prep time: 20 minutes | Cook time: 20 minutes | Serves 3

2 teaspoons olive oil
2 boneless skinless chicken breasts, cut into bite-size pieces
2 garlic cloves, minced
1 cup chicken stock
2 lemons, zested, and juiced

1 teaspoon lemon pepper seasoning
½ teaspoon dried basil
½ teaspoon dried oregano
Salt and freshly ground black pepper, to taste
1 tablespoon cornstarch
2 tablespoons cold water

1. Heat olive oil in a large nonstick skillet over medium heat and sauté chicken just until cooked through, 7 to 8 minutes, stirring frequently. Add garlic and sauté about 1 minute more, stirring constantly. 2. Add chicken stock, lemon juice, lemon pepper, basil and oregano to chicken mixture and season to taste with salt and pepper. Reduce heat and simmer until chicken is cooked through and liquid is slightly reduced, 7 to 8 minutes, stirring occasionally. 3. Whisk cornstarch into cold water, add to skillet and stir gently until combined. Simmer until sauce is thickened, about 2 minutes, stirring constantly. 4. Transfer lemon chicken to a large bowl, sprinkle with lemon zest and serve immediately. Enjoy!

Per Serving

calories: 134 | fat: 5g | protein: 18g | carbs: 8g | fiber: 1g | sugar: 2g | sodium: 321mg

Chicken Curry Wraps

Prep time: 10 minutes | Cook time: 0 minutes | Serves 2

1 cup cooked diced chicken
½ cup plain unsweetened yogurt
1 tablespoon skim milk, plus more if needed
1 celery stalk, diced
½ teaspoon curry powder
¼ teaspoon onion powder
Salt and freshly ground black pepper, to taste
2 large green lettuce leaves
1 tablespoon slivered almonds, toasted

1. Mix chicken, yogurt, milk, celery, curry powder and onion powder and season to taste with salt and pepper. 2. Spread chicken mixture on lettuce leaves and sprinkle with almonds. 3. Roll up lettuce leaves burrito-style over chicken mixture. Serve immediately and enjoy!

Per Serving

calories: 148 | fat: 5g | protein: 23g | carbs: 3g | fiber: 1g | sugar: 2g | sodium: 358mg

Chicken Caprese

Prep time: 15 minutes | Cook time: 15 minutes | Serves 4

1 pound (454 g) boneless skinless chicken breasts
2 tablespoons olive oil, divided
1 teaspoon garlic powder
1 teaspoon onion powder
1 teaspoon Italian herb seasoning
Salt and freshly ground black pepper, to taste
½ cup grated mozzarella cheese
1 cup halved cherry tomatoes
2 tablespoons balsamic vinegar
2 tablespoons sliced fresh basil leaves

1. Cut chicken breasts lengthwise into 1-inch thick slices and brush all over with about 1 tablespoon olive oil. Mix garlic powder, onion powder and herb seasoning, sprinkle over chicken and season to taste with salt and pepper. 2. Heat remaining 1 tablespoon olive oil in a large nonstick skillet over medium heat and cook chicken until lightly golden brown and no longer pink inside, 8 to 10 minutes, turning as necessary. Sprinkle mozzarella cheese over chicken and cook until cheese is melted, about 1 minute more. 3. Transfer chicken to a serving plate and arrange tomatoes over chicken. Drizzle balsamic vinegar over chicken, sprinkle with basil and serve immediately. Enjoy!

Per Serving

calories: 234 | fat: 10g | protein: 31g | carbs: 4g | fiber: 1g | sugar: 2g | sodium: 161mg

Creamy Pepper Chicken Skillet

Prep time: 10 minutes | Cook time: 15 minutes | Serves 4

Low-fat cooking spray
1 onion, sliced
4 bell peppers (red, green, yellow, or orange, or a mixture), cored, seeded, and thinly sliced
1 pound (454 g) skinless and boneless chicken breasts, or chicken tenders, cut into strips
¼ cup light cream cheese (with herbs, if desired)
Salt and freshly ground black pepper

1. Generously spray a nonstick pan or skillet with low-fat cooking spray. Heat, add the onion and bell peppers, and cook for 5 to 7 minutes, until softened, stirring occasionally. Remove from the pan and keep warm. 2. Add the chicken and a little extra spray, if necessary, and cook until no longer pink, about 3 to 4 minutes each side. 3. Return the pepper mixture to the pan and mix well. Add the cream cheese and season with salt and pepper, and cook for 1 to 2 minutes, or until the cheese has melted and the sauce is creamy. 4. Serve hot with rice, pasta, or vegetables of your choice.

Per Serving

calories: 205 | fat: 3g | protein: 34g | carbs: 11g | fiber: 3g | sugar: 5g | sodium: 245mg

DZ's Grilled Chicken Wings

Prep time: 15 minutes | Cook time: 20 minutes | Makes about 18 wings

1½ pounds (680 g) frozen chicken wings
Freshly ground black pepper
1 teaspoon garlic powder

1 cup buffalo wing sauce, such as Frank's RedHot
1 teaspoon extra-virgin olive oil

1. Preheat the grill to 350°F (180°C). 2. Season the wings with the black pepper and garlic powder. 3. Grill the wings for 15 minutes per side. They will be browned and crispy when finished. 4. Toss the grilled wings in the buffalo wing sauce and olive oil. 5. Serve immediately.

Per Serving (1 wing)
calories: 82 | fat: 6g | protein: 7g | carbs: 1g | fiber: 0g | sugar: 0g | sodium: 400mg

Almond-Crusted Chicken Tenders

Prep time: 10 minutes | Cook time: 35 minutes | Serves 4

Nonstick cooking spray
¾ cup almond flour, divided
¼ cup cornstarch

½ teaspoon salt
2 large eggs
16 ounces (454 g) boneless, skinless chicken tenders

1. Preheat the oven to 400°F (205°C). Coat a baking sheet with nonstick cooking spray or parchment paper. 2. While the oven preheats, prepare one plate with ½ cup almond flour, and a second plate with ¼ cup almond flour, cornstarch, and salt. In a small bowl, beat the eggs. 3. With the baking sheet next to your prepping station, coat each side of each chicken tender with the cornstarch and almond flour mixture first, then coat well in egg, and finally coat with the almond flour. Place the battered tender on the baking sheet. Repeat this process for all chicken tenders. 4. Bake for about 35 minutes, turning the tenders over at the halfway point of cooking time, when the batter begins to brown. Serve immediately. 5. Store leftovers in an airtight container in the refrigerator up to 3 days. When reheating, place in oven at 350°F (180°C) for 7 to 10 minutes to restore the crispiness of the batter.

Per Serving
calories: 296 | fat: 14g | protein: 31g | carbs: 12g | fiber: 2g | sugar: 1g | sodium: 597mg

Chicken Breasts Stuffed with Ham and Cheese

Prep time: 10 minutes | Cook time: 15 minutes | Serves 4

1 pound (454 g) chicken breast cutlets, pounded very thinly
4 ounces (113 g) lean boiled ham, sliced thinly (4 slices)
4 ounces (113 g) low-fat Swiss cheese, sliced thinly (4 slices)
Cooking spray
1 cup thinly sliced fresh mushrooms

1 large shallot, finely minced
½ cup dry white wine
¼ cup fat-free, low-sodium chicken broth
1 teaspoon dried tarragon
Salt and pepper, to taste

1. Cut pounded chicken into eight thin cutlets. Lay out four cutlets; top each with a slice of ham and a slice of cheese, and then top each with a second cutlet. 2. Coat a large nonstick skillet with cooking spray and sauté stuffed chicken cutlets over medium-high heat, carefully turning once, for 8 to 10 minutes, until golden and cooked through. Transfer to a plate and keep warm. 3. Re-spray pan and sauté mushrooms and shallot over medium-high heat, stirring, for 3 minutes. Add wine to deglaze pan, stirring to scrape up any browned bits, and simmer until it's reduced by half. 4. Add chicken broth and tarragon and simmer for 2 minutes. Stir in any chicken juices that have accumulated on plate and add salt and pepper to taste.

Per Serving
calories: 272 | fat: 6g | protein: 42g | carbs: 6g | fiber: 1g | sugar: 2g | sodium: 385mg

Baked Garlic-Greek Yogurt Chicken with Parmesan

Prep time: 10 minutes | Cook time: 45 minutes | Serves 4

Nonstick cooking spray
1 cup low-fat plain Greek yogurt
½ cup shredded Parmesan cheese
1½ teaspoons seasoning salt
1 teaspoon garlic powder
½ teaspoon freshly ground black pepper
4 (4-ounce / 113-g) boneless, skinless chicken breasts

1. Preheat the oven to 375°F (190°C). Coat a 9-by-13-inch baking dish with cooking spray and set aside. 2. In a small bowl, mix to combine the yogurt, cheese, salt, garlic powder, and pepper. 3. Place the chicken breasts in the baking dish. 4. Use a pastry or marinade brush to coat each breast with the yogurt mixture. 5. Bake for 45 minutes, or until the juices run clear and the topping begins to brown, and serve.

Per Serving
calories: 273 | fat: 8g | protein: 45g | carbs: 3g | fiber: 0g | sugar: 2g | sodium: 519mg

One-Pan Chicken and Broccoli

Prep time: 10 minutes | Cook time: 20 minutes | Serves 8

1 tablespoon extra-virgin olive oil
1 yellow onion, chopped
2 teaspoons minced garlic
1 pound (454 g) boneless, skinless chicken breast, cooked and diced
1 cup water
1 cup chicken broth
1 cup quinoa
½ teaspoon dried thyme
2½ cups chopped broccoli

1. In a medium skillet over medium heat, heat the olive oil. Add the onion and garlic, and sauté until the onion is soft, 2 to 3 minutes. 2. Add the chicken, water, broth, quinoa, and thyme. Bring the liquid to a boil, cover, reduce the heat to medium-low, and cook for 10 minutes. 3. Add the broccoli, cover, and cook for 7 minutes more, until the quinoa fluffs with a fork and the broccoli is tender.

Per Serving (1 cup)
calories: 176 | fat: 4g | protein: 17g | carbs: 17g | fiber: 3g | sugar: 1g | sodium: 323mg

Chicken Burgers with Scallions and Ginger

Prep time: 5 minutes | Cook time: 20 minutes | Serves 4

Extra-virgin olive oil, for greasing the pan
⅓ cup thinly sliced scallions
3 tablespoons soy sauce
2 tablespoons minced peeled ginger
1 pound (454 g) lean ground chicken

1. Preheat the oven to 375°F (190°C). Lightly coat a baking sheet with olive oil and set aside. 2. In a large bowl, mix the scallions, soy sauce, and ginger until well combined. 3. Add the chicken to the sauce mix and gently combine, making sure not to overmix. 4. Evenly separate the meat mixture into four sections, then form the sections into patties and place on the baking sheet. Cook for 10 minutes, then flip and cook for another 10 minutes, until the patties are fully cooked and the internal temperature of each has reached 165°F (74°C). Serve hot.

Per Serving
calories: 181 | fat: 9g | protein: 23g | carbs: 2g | fiber: 1g | sugar: 1g | sodium: 713mg

Skillet Sausage with Peppers and Onions

Prep time: 5 minutes | Cook time: 25 minutes | Serves 4

1 tablespoon extra-virgin olive oil
2 bell peppers, seeded and sliced
1 white onion, sliced

4 tablespoons white wine, divided
4 garlic cloves, minced
5 lean chicken sausage links, sliced diagonally

1. In a large nonstick skillet over medium-low heat, warm the olive oil. Add the peppers, onion, 3 tablespoons of white wine, and garlic and cook for about 10 minutes, until the vegetables are tender. Remove from the pan and set aside. 2. In the same skillet, combine the chicken sausage and remaining 1 tablespoon white wine and raise the heat to medium. Cook for about 10 minutes, stirring periodically, until golden brown. 3. Place the cooked pepper mixture back in the skillet with the chicken sausage and toss to combine and heat through, about 5 minutes. Serve hot.

Per Serving

calories: 184 | fat: 9g | protein: 14g | carbs: 11g | fiber: 2g | sugar: 3g | sodium: 453mg

Turkey Cutlets Francese

Prep time: 10 minutes | Cook time: 10 minutes | Serves 4

½ cup grated Parmesan cheese
¼ cup dried parsley flakes
1 cup egg substitute
¼ cup skim milk

1 pound (454 g) turkey cutlets, thinly sliced
Olive oil cooking spray
½ cup white wine
2 tablespoons concentrated chicken broth

1. On a flat plate, mix Parmesan cheese and parsley. 2. In a baking dish or platter with sides, mix eggs and milk. Dip cutlets into egg, then into cheese mixture, then back into egg. 3. Coat a nonstick skillet with cooking spray and heat over medium-high heat until hot but not smoking. Sauté cutlets for 3 minutes on each side, or until browned. Transfer to a plate and keep warm. 4. Lower heat to low, pour wine into pan, and simmer, stirring to scrape up any browned bits. 5. Add concentrated chicken broth and continue to simmer, stirring, for 2 more minutes, or until sauce reduces slightly.

Per Serving

calories: 217 | fat: 6g | protein: 36g | carbs: 4g | fiber: 0g | sugar: 2g | sodium: 490mg

Turkey Cacciatore

Prep time: 10 minutes | Cook time: 35 minutes | Serves 4

Olive oil cooking spray
1 pound (454 g) skinless, boneless turkey thighs (or any dark turkey meat)
1 cup chopped onion
2 garlic cloves, minced
2 tablespoons sun-dried tomato paste

1 (14½-ounce / 411-g) can whole tomatoes
¼ cup chopped fresh basil
1 teaspoon dried oregano
¼ teaspoon red pepper flakes
½ cup dry red wine
Salt and pepper, to taste

1. Heat cooking spray in a large nonstick pot over medium-high heat until hot but not smoking. Cook turkey for 3 minutes until browned all over and remove from pot. 2. Add onion and garlic and sauté for 2 minutes, or until lightly browned. Add tomato paste and cook, stirring, until paste starts to darken. 3. Put turkey back into pot, add all other ingredients, and stir well. 4. Cover, lower heat to low, and simmer for 30 minutes until turkey is tender.

Per Serving

calories: 217 | fat: 5g | protein: 26g | carbs: 15g | fiber: 3g | sugar: 6g | sodium: 256mg

Turkey Curry

Prep time: 15 minutes | Cook time: 20 minutes | Serves 4

Canola oil or other neutral-flavor cooking spray
1 medium yellow onion, chopped
3 garlic cloves, minced
1 pound (454 g) skinless, boneless turkey breast, cut into 1-inch cubes
1 tablespoon grated fresh ginger, or 1½ teaspoons ground
1 teaspoon sweet paprika
1 teaspoon curry powder
½ teaspoon ground cumin
½ teaspoon ground cinnamon
1 (15-ounce / 425-g) can low-sodium crushed tomatoes
½ cup unsweetened light coconut milk
½ cup plain, fat-free yogurt
½ cup golden raisins, roughly chopped

1. Spray a large skillet with cooking spray. Heat over medium-high heat until it shimmers. 2. Add onion and garlic and cook until soft, about 4 minutes. 3. Stir in turkey breast and cook until golden all over, 3 to 5 minutes. 4. Sprinkle turkey mixture with spices, then add tomatoes and coconut milk, lower heat, and simmer for 5 to 7 minutes. 5. Stir in yogurt and raisins and simmer for 5 more minutes.

Per Serving
calories: 225 | fat: 1g | protein: 30g | carbs: 29g | fiber: 4g | sugar: 6g | sodium: 209mg

Baked Turkey Meatballs

Prep time: 15 minutes | Cook time: 20 minutes | Makes 12 meatballs

Nonstick cooking spray
1 egg
16 to 20 ounces (454 to 567 g) ground turkey breast
½ cup old-fashioned oats
1 small onion, chopped
2 tablespoons Worcestershire sauce
1 tablespoon tomato paste
1 teaspoon freshly ground black pepper

1. Preheat the oven to 350ºF (180ºC). Coat the cups of a 12-cup muffin tin with cooking spray. 2. In a small bowl, lightly whisk the egg. 3. In a large bowl, mix together the ground turkey, oats, onion, Worcestershire sauce, tomato paste, pepper, and egg. 4. Using clean hands, shape the turkey mixture into 12 equal-size meatballs and place one in each muffin cup. 5. Bake for 20 minutes, or until the meat is cooked thoroughly and a meat thermometer reads 165ºF (74ºC), and serve.

Per Serving (1 meatball)
calories: 81 | fat: 1g | protein: 10g | carbs: 8g | fiber: 0g | sugar: 2g | sodium: 254mg

Chapter 11 Pork, Beef and Lamb

133 Cupboard Chorizo and Bean Hotpot   72
134 Pork Egg Roll Bowls   72
135 Mozzarella-Stuffed Meatballs   72
136 Indonesian Braised Pork   73
137 Braised Pork Tenderloin   73
138 Pork with Onions and Capers   73
139 Cider-Glazed Pork Chops   74
140 Flank Steak Basquaise   74
141 Bell Pepper Nachos   74
142 Gingered Ham   75
143 Greek Lamb Burgers with Yogurt-Mint Sauce   75
144 Peppercorn and Mustard Crusted Lamb Chops   76
145 Mom's Sloppy Joes   76
146 Pan-Grilled Burgers with Blue Cheese   76
147 Spiced Lamb Chops   77

Cupboard Chorizo and Bean Hotpot

Prep time: 10 minutes | Cook time: 15 minutes | Serves 4

4 ounces (113 g) cured chorizo sausage, skinned and chopped
3 red onions, chopped
3 garlic cloves, crushed
1 teaspoon smoked paprika
1 (14-ounce / 397-g) can diced tomatoes
2 (14-ounce / 397-g) cans lima beans, drained and rinsed
Salt and freshly ground black pepper

1. Cook the chorizo, onions, and garlic in a large frying pan until the oil begins to run. Continue to sauté over a gentle heat, stirring occasionally, until the onions are soft. 2. Add the smoked paprika, tomatoes, and lima beans, mixing well. Stir and simmer over low heat for about 10 minutes. 3. Season to taste with salt and pepper, then spoon into dishes to serve, with bread to mop up the spicy juices, if desired.

Per Serving
calories: 270 | fat: 9g | protein: 17g | carbs: 32g | fiber: 10g | sugar: 11g | sodium: 302mg

Pork Egg Roll Bowls

Prep time: 5 minutes | Cook time: 25 minutes | Serves 4

2 tablespoons toasted sesame oil, divided
1 pound (454 g) extra-lean ground pork
1 (14-ounce / 397-g) package coleslaw mix
2 tablespoons seasoned rice wine vinegar
2 tablespoons low-sodium soy sauce
1 tablespoon water, if needed

1. In a large nonstick skillet over medium-high heat, warm 1 tablespoon sesame oil. 2. Add the pork to the skillet and cook for about 10 minutes, until the pork is totally cooked through and no pink remains. Remove from the heat and set aside in a bowl. 3. In the same skillet, reduce the heat to medium and warm the remaining 1 tablespoon sesame oil. 4. Add the coleslaw mix and toss to coat in the oil, then add the rice wine vinegar and soy sauce. Cook, stirring occasionally, for about 10 minutes, until the coleslaw mix is very soft and reduced in volume. If it seems too dry, add 1 tablespoon of water. 5. Once the coleslaw mix is cooked and reduced in volume by about half, add the cooked pork back to the skillet and toss to combine. Cook for another 5 minutes to let the flavors meld. Serve hot.

Per Serving
calories: 248 | fat: 12g | protein: 26g | carbs: 9g | fiber: 2g | sugar: 6g | sodium: 455mg

Mozzarella-Stuffed Meatballs

Prep time: 10 minutes | Cook time: 20 minutes | Serves 4

1 tablespoon extra-virgin olive oil
1 pound (454 g) 95 percent lean ground beef
1 tablespoon garlic powder
1 tablespoon granulated onion
Salt
Freshly ground black pepper
2 (1-ounce / 28-g) pieces low-fat mozzarella string cheese
1 (20-ounce / 567-g) jar tomato sauce

1. Preheat the oven to 375ºF (190ºC). Line a baking sheet with aluminum foil, coat with the olive oil, and set aside. 2. In a large bowl, combine the ground beef with the garlic powder and granulated onion. Season with salt and pepper and mix to combine. 3. Cut each piece of string cheese into 5 equal portions and set aside. 4. Separate the meat into 10 equal portions. Pick up a portion and flatten it a bit to accommodate a piece of string cheese. Roll the meat around the cheese into a ball and place it onto the baking sheet. 5. Roll the meatball around on the baking sheet to lightly coat with olive oil. Repeat with the remaining meat and cheese. 6. Bake for about 20 minutes, flipping the meatballs halfway through, or until the beef reaches an internal temperature of 160ºF (71ºC) and is no longer pink inside. 7. While the meatballs are baking, in a small pot over low heat, warm the tomato sauce until it just barely bubbles. 8. Remove the meatballs from the oven. Top the meatballs with the warm tomato sauce and serve hot.

Per Serving
calories: 315 | fat: 11g | protein: 30g | carbs: 20g | fiber: 4g | sugar: 9g | sodium: 558mg

Indonesian Braised Pork

Prep time: 10 minutes | Cook time: 5 minutes | Serves 4

1 pound (454 g) lean pork tenderloin
Canola cooking spray
½ cup chopped shallots
½ teaspoon Asian chili paste with garlic
1 tablespoon minced fresh ginger
1½ tablespoons light soy sauce
1 cup light unsweetened coconut milk
2 tablespoons fresh lime juice

1. Slice tenderloin in ½-inch-thick slices. 2. In a medium nonstick lidded skillet, heat cooking spray over medium-high heat. Brown pork for about 1 minute on each side. Add shallots and sauté until golden. 3. In a small bowl, mix chili paste, ginger, soy sauce, and coconut milk. Add to pan, cover, then lower heat and simmer, turning meat occasionally, for about 2 minutes, or until it is cooked through. 4. Add lime juice, stir, and simmer for 1 more minute.

Per Serving
calories: 318 | fat: 9g | protein: 28g | carbs: 10g | fiber: 0g | sugar: 3g | sodium: 254mg

Braised Pork Tenderloin

Prep time: 10 minutes | Cook time: 20 minutes | Serves 4

1½ cups chopped leeks, rinsed well
1 cup dry white wine
1 tablespoon Dijon mustard
Brown-sugar artificial sweetener (1 teaspoon equivalent)
2 garlic cloves, minced
¼ tablespoon ground thyme
1 tablespoon prepared horseradish
Salt and pepper, to taste
1 pound (454 g) lean pork tenderloin
Canola cooking spray

1. In a large bowl, combine leeks, ½ cup of wine, mustard, sweetener, garlic, thyme, horseradish, salt, and pepper and pour into a large resealable plastic bag. 2. Add pork tenderloin to bag, seal it, and shake to coat completely. Chill in refrigerator for 2½ hours. 3. Remove pork from bag, reserving marinade. Coat bottom of large nonstick lidded skillet with cooking spray and heat over medium-high heat until hot but not smoking. Sear pork for 2 minutes on each side. 4. Pour remaining ½ cup of wine into reserved marinade in bag, shake well, and pour over pork. 5. Lower heat to medium-low, cover skillet, and braise for 15 to 20 minutes, or until pork is cooked through. Remove pork, slice thinly, and keep warm. 6. Simmer sauce for 3 minutes to reduce slightly.

Per Serving
calories: 200 | fat: 8g | protein: 21g | carbs: 8g | fiber: 1g | sugar: 2g | sodium: 130mg

Pork with Onions and Capers

Prep time: 10 minutes | Cook time: 10 minutes | Serves 4

1 pound (454 g) pork tenderloin
Butter-flavored cooking spray
1½ cups thinly sliced onion
½ cup dry vermouth
¼ cup water
2 teaspoons concentrated chicken broth
2 tablespoons capers
¼ cup fat-free sour cream
Salt and pepper, to taste

1. Slice tenderloin into ½-inch slices. 2. In a large nonstick skillet, heat cooking spray over medium-high heat until hot but not smoking. Sauté pork for about 2 minutes on each side, then remove from pan. 3. Re-spray pan and add onion. Cook, stirring, for 3 to 4 minutes, or until onion just starts to brown. 4. Add vermouth and water and simmer for 3 to 4 minutes, or until liquid is reduced to about ¼ cup. 5. Stir in concentrated chicken broth and capers. Increase heat to high and bring onion mixture to a boil, then cook until reduced by half. 6. Turn off heat, stir in sour cream, and add sliced pork and any accumulated meat juices back to skillet. Turn pork slices to coat, and serve. Salt and pepper, to taste.

Per Serving
calories: 218 | fat: 6g | protein: 26g | carbs: 9g | fiber: 1g | sugar: 2g | sodium: 286mg

Cider-Glazed Pork Chops

Prep time: 5 minutes | Cook time: 12 minutes | Serves 4

Butter-flavored cooking spray
1 pound (454 g) lean boneless pork chops
1 cup apple cider
Brown-sugar artificial sweetener (1 teaspoon equivalent)

1 teaspoon Dijon mustard
½ cup fat-free, low-sodium chicken broth
2 tablespoons cider vinegar

1. In a medium nonstick skillet, heat cooking spray over medium-high heat until hot but not smoking. Sauté pork for 2 minutes on one side, turn, and cook for 2 minutes on the other, then remove chops and keep warm. 2. Stir together cider and sweetener and add to skillet. Simmer, uncovered, for 1 minute; then add mustard, broth, and vinegar, stirring to scrape up any browned bits. Simmer for 5 minutes, or until sauce is slightly thickened. 3. Return chops to pan with any meat juices that have accumulated and turn chops in sauce to coat. Simmer for 2 more minutes over low heat, then serve.

Per Serving

calories: 161 | fat: 4g | protein: 26g | carbs: 6g | fiber: 0g | sugar: 1g | sodium: 189mg

Flank Steak Basquaise

Prep time: 10 minutes | Cook time: 13 minutes | Serves 4

Olive oil cooking spray
1 pound (454 g) lean flank steak
½ cup chopped onion
2 garlic cloves, chopped
½ cup seeded and chopped red bell pepper

½ pound (227 g) sliced fresh mushrooms
½ cup dry red wine
½ cup chopped plum tomatoes
2 teaspoons concentrated beef broth
Salt and pepper, to taste

1. Preheat broiler and arrange rack to top position. 2. Spray broiler pan with cooking spray and place flank steak on top. With a sharp knife, score top of steak so it won't curl. Broil for 3 to 5 minutes on each side, or until medium rare. 3. While steak is broiling, heat cooking spray in a medium nonstick skillet over medium-high heat until it's hot but not smoking. Sauté onion and garlic for 3 minutes, or until lightly browned. 4. Add bell pepper and mushrooms and cook, covered, for 3 to 5 minutes, or until soft. Add wine, tomatoes, and beef broth concentrate and cook, stirring occasionally, until liquid is reduced by half. 5. Slice steak very thinly on diagonal. Add salt and pepper to taste. Spoon vegetable-wine sauce on top.

Per Serving

calories: 186 | fat: 6g | protein: 27g | carbs: 5g | fiber: 1g | sugar: 2g | sodium: 167mg

Bell Pepper Nachos

Prep time: 10 minutes | Cook time: 20 minutes | Serves 4

1 pound (454 g) 93% lean ground beef
⅓ cup salsa
2 tablespoons Taco seasoning

Nonstick cooking spray
20 to 25 mini bell peppers, halved lengthwise, trimmed, and seeded

1. 1 cup Mexican shredded cheese. 2. 1.Preheat the oven to 400ºF (205ºC). 3. 2.In a large skillet over medium heat, brown the meat until no longer pink, breaking it up as it cooks, 7 to 10 minutes. Drain the meat, and stir in the salsa and Taco seasoning. Simmer for 3 to 5 minutes, until the liquid has cooked down. 4. 3.Spray a large baking sheet with cooking spray and arrange the peppers on the sheet cut-side up. 5. 4.Fill the peppers with the beef, and sprinkle with the cheese. 6. 5.Bake until the cheese is melted, about 5 minutes, and serve immediately.

Per Serving

calories: 348 | fat: 17g | protein: 31g | carbs: 15g | fiber: 2g | sugar: 7g | sodium: 526mg

Gingered Ham

Prep time: 10 minutes | Cook time: 5 hours | Serves 8

6½ pounds (2.9 kg) boneless ham
2½ cups sugar-free ginger beer
1 onion, quartered
Small piece ginger, peeled and sliced
10 black peppercorns
6 whole cloves
1 tablespoon grated peeled fresh ginger
3 tablespoons reduced-sugar ginger jam, jelly, or marmalade, or orange marmalade
Extra cloves, to decorate (optional)

1. Preheat the oven to 320ºF (160ºC). Place the ham in a deep roasting pan that will snugly hold it. Add all but ⅓ cup of the ginger beer to the ham along with the onion, sliced ginger, peppercorns, and cloves. Cover tightly with a double layer of foil and bake for 4½ hours, basting once or twice. 2. Uncover and pour away all but 1 tablespoon of the juices from the ham. Increase the oven temperature to 400ºF (205ºC). Make the Glaze: 3. Heat the remaining ginger beer with the grated ginger and ginger jam, until boiling. Reduce the heat and simmer for 5 minutes, until syrupy. 4. Meanwhile, cut away any skin from the ham, leaving just a thin layer of fat. Score the fat into a diamond pattern and brush over half the glaze. Decorate the cut surface with studded cloves, if desired. Return to the oven and roast, uncovered, for 10 minutes. 5. Brush again with the remaining glaze, and roast for a further 10 to 15 minutes, until golden. Serve hot or cold.

Per Serving

calories: 470 | fat: 23g | protein: 62g | carbs: 3g | fiber: 1g | sugar: 1g | sodium: 439mg

Greek Lamb Burgers with Yogurt-Mint Sauce

Prep time: 20 minutes | Cook time: 8 minutes | Serves 4

Burgers:
3 or 4 scallions (white and light green parts only), chopped (about ¾ cup)
1 pound (454 g) lean ground lamb
1 teaspoon ground cumin

Yogurt-Mint Sauce:
½ teaspoon fresh lemon zest
½ cup fresh mint leaves
1 small garlic clove, quartered
¾ cup plain, fat-free yogurt

1 teaspoon ground coriander
Salt and pepper, to taste
Olive oil cooking spray

1 teaspoon ground cumin
1 tablespoon fresh lemon juice
2 teaspoons concentrated chicken broth

1. Mix scallions, lamb, and seasonings in bowl so they are well blended. Divide and form into four patties. 2. In a medium nonstick skillet, heat cooking spray over medium-high heat until hot but not smoking. Place patties in skillet and cook for 4 minutes, then turn over and cook for 4 minutes more for medium rare. 3. While meat is cooking, combine lemon zest, mint, and garlic in mini-processor or chopper and finely chop. 4. In a medium-size bowl, mix yogurt, cumin, lemon juice, and concentrated chicken broth. Add chopped mint mixture and mix well. 5. Remove burgers from skillet and drain on paper towels. Serve burgers with sauce spooned on top.

Per Serving

calories: 346 | fat: 27g | protein: 21g | carbs: 8g | fiber: 2g | sugar: 3g | sodium: 156mg

Peppercorn and Mustard Crusted Lamb Chops

Prep time: 10 minutes | Cook time: 30 minutes | Serves 4

2 tablespoons mixed or black whole peppercorns, coarsely ground
2 tablespoons whole-grain mustard
3 tablespoons bottled minced roasted garlic
4 lamb chops, ½ inch thick, well trimmed of fat
Olive oil cooking spray
1 cup low-sodium beef broth
2 tablespoons fresh lemon juice
½ teaspoon dried mint
½ cup reduced-fat sour cream

1. Preheat oven to 375ºF (190ºC). 2. Combine ground peppercorns, mustard, and garlic to form a paste. Spread all over chops. 3. Spray a baking dish with olive oil spray. Place chops in dish and bake for 15 to 17 minutes. 4. While chops are baking, combine broth, lemon juice, and mint in a small saucepan and bring to a boil, then lower heat and simmer for about 15 minutes. 5. Turn off heat. Add sour cream to broth mixture and stir until smooth. Serve with lamb chops.

Per Serving
calories: 110 | fat: 4g | protein: 11g | carbs: 10g | fiber: 1g | sugar: 0g | sodium: 384mg

Mom's Sloppy Joes

Prep time: 10 minutes | Cook time: 30 minutes | Serves 8

Nonstick cooking spray
1½ pounds (680 g) supreme lean ground beef
1 cup chopped onion
1 cup chopped celery
1 (8-ounce / 227-g) can tomato sauce
⅓ cup catsup (without high-fructose corn syrup)
2 tablespoons white vinegar
2 tablespoons Worcestershire sauce
2 tablespoons Dijon mustard
1 tablespoon brown sugar
8 100% whole-grain thin sandwich rolls, such as Thomas' sandwich thins (optional)

1. Spray a large skillet with cooking spray, and place it over medium heat. Add the beef and cook until it is no longer pink, about 10 minutes. Drain off any grease. 2. Mix in the onion and celery, and cook for 2 to 3 minutes. 3. Stir in the tomato sauce, catsup, vinegar, Worcestershire sauce, mustard, and brown sugar. Bring the liquid to a simmer, and reduce the heat to low. Cook for 15 minutes, or until the sauce has thickened. 4. Toast the sandwich rolls (if using), spoon about ¾ cup of sloppy joe onto each roll or plate, and serve.

Per Serving
calories: 269 | fat: 5g | protein: 24g | carbs: 32g | fiber: 6g | sugar: 6g | sodium: 586mg

Pan-Grilled Burgers with Blue Cheese

Prep time: 10 minutes | Cook time: 8 minutes | Serves 4

1 pound (454 g) lean ground beef
2 tablespoons steak or beef rub (I use Penzeys English Prime Rib Rub)
Butter-flavored cooking spray
½ cup reduced-fat sour cream
1 tablespoon prepared horseradish
2 teaspoons Bovrite or other condensed beef broth
1 tablespoon crumbled blue cheese

1. Divide and shape meat into four 1-inch-thick patties. Sprinkle steak rub on both sides of patties and press so that seasoning sticks to meat. 2. Heat a heavy skillet over medium-high heat until very hot and spray with cooking spray. Cook patties for 4 minutes on one side, flip, and cook for 4 minutes on other side. 3. While burgers are cooking, mix sour cream, horseradish, and condensed beef broth in small bowl. Add blue cheese and stir until combined.

Per Serving
calories: 182 | fat: 7g | protein: 26g | carbs: 6g | fiber: 0g | sugar: 2g | sodium: 319mg

Spiced Lamb Chops

Prep time: 10 minutes | Cook time: 8 minutes | Serves 4

2 garlic cloves, finely minced
¼ teaspoon ground cumin
¼ teaspoon ground cardamom
2 tablespoons water
1 teaspoon concentrated chicken broth
1 pound (454 g) shoulder lamb chops (about 4), ½ inch thick, well trimmed of fat
Olive oil cooking spray
¾ cup plain, fat-free yogurt
1 tablespoon fresh lime juice
Salt and pepper, to taste

1. In a shallow dish, stir together garlic, cumin, cardamom, water, and concentrated chicken broth. Dip lamb chops in mixture, turning once to coat well. Cover with foil and marinate at room temperature for 15 minutes. 2. Coat a large nonstick skillet with cooking spray and heat over medium-high heat until hot but not smoking. Reserving marinade, remove lamb chops from marinade. Cook lamb chops for about 3 minutes on each side for medium rare. Transfer lamb to a platter and keep warm. 3. Add yogurt and lime juice to reserved marinade, pour into skillet, lower heat to low, and simmer for 5 minutes, or until cooked through and slightly reduced. Add salt and pepper to taste.

Per Serving

calories: 191 | fat: 8g | protein: 25g | carbs: 5g | fiber: 0g | sugar: 4g | sodium: 123mg

Chapter 12 Fish and Seafood

148 Herbed Salmon   79

149 Bluefish with Mustard-Horseradish Glaze   79

150 Salmon Croquettes with Spicy Tartar Sauce   79

151 Southwest Salmon and Roasted Red Onion and Peppers   80

152 Tangy Swordfish and Tomatoes   80

153 Souvlaki-Style Swordfish   80

154 Seared Tuna over Sesame Spinach   81

155 Crispy Baked Cod   81

156 Mahi-Mahi with Mango-Avocado Salsa   81

157 Mustard-Crusted Halibut   82

158 Crispy Baked Coconut Shrimp   82

159 Smoky Fish Frittata   82

160 Cajun-Spiced Catfish with Citrus-Horseradish Sauce   83

161 Balinese Shrimp   83

162 Zesty Lime Shrimp with Avocado   83

163 Classic Crab-Stuffed Tomatoes   84

164 Lemon-Parsley Crab Cakes   84

165 Scallops Provençale   84

166 Scallops Piquant   85

167 Coquilles Saint-Jacques   85

Herbed Salmon

Prep time: 10 minutes | Cook time: 15 minutes | Serves 2

2 salmon fillets
½ teaspoon onion powder
½ teaspoon garlic powder
Salt and freshly ground black pepper, to taste
1 tablespoon olive oil
1 (14-ounce / 397-g) can diced tomatoes
1 teaspoon Italian herb seasoning
2 tablespoons finely grated Parmesan cheese

1. Preheat a medium nonstick skillet over medium heat. Brush salmon fillets with olive oil, sprinkle with onion and garlic powder and season to taste with salt and pepper. Sear fillets until browned on both sides, turning as necessary, 3 to 4 minutes 2. Pour undrained tomatoes over salmon fillets, sprinkle with herb seasoning and season to taste with salt and pepper. Heat to a boil, then reduce heat, cover and simmer until salmon is cooked through, 6 to 8 minutes. 3. Transfer salmon with sauce onto plates and sprinkle with Parmesan cheese to serve. Enjoy!

Per Serving

calories: 238 | fat: 10g | protein: 30g | carbs: 7g | fiber: 2g | sugar: 4g | sodium: 333mg

Bluefish with Mustard-Horseradish Glaze

Prep time: 10 minutes | Cook time: 9 minutes | Serves 4

1 pound (454 g) bluefish fillets
Olive oil cooking spray
¼ cup light mayonnaise
1 tablespoon prepared horseradish
2 tablespoons Dijon mustard
¼ cup minced shallots
2 teaspoons Worcestershire sauce
2 tablespoons minced dried parsley, plus more for serving

1. Preheat broiler and arrange rack to top position. Place fillets, skin side down, in broiling pan and coat lightly with cooking spray. 2. Broil bluefish for 6 minutes, or until almost done. 3. While fish is broiling, combine mayonnaise, horseradish, mustard, shallots, Worcestershire, and parsley in a small bowl. 4. Remove fish from broiler, spread lightly with sauce, and continue to broil for about 3 minutes, or until lightly browned. Sprinkle with parsley and serve.

Per Serving

calories: 202 | fat: 10g | protein: 24g | carbs: 3g | fiber: 1g | sugar: 1g | sodium: 258mg

Salmon Croquettes with Spicy Tartar Sauce

Prep time: 15 minutes | Cook time: 15 minutes | Serves 4

1 (14-ounce / 397-g) can pink salmon, drained
¼ cup gluten-free unseasoned panko crispy (Japanese-style bread crumbs)
½ cup egg substitute or 1 large egg, lightly beaten
2 tablespoons low-fat mayonnaise
1 tablespoon dried minced parsley
2 tablespoons dried minced onion
1 tablespoon dried celery leaves
1 teaspoon Worcestershire sauce
Olive oil cooking spray
Spicy Tartar Sauce:
½ cup low-fat mayonnaise
1 tablespoon sweet pickle relish
1 teaspoon fresh lemon juice
1 teaspoon prepared horseradish
½ teaspoon lemon-pepper

1. In a medium bowl, combine salmon with panko, egg substitute or egg, mayonnaise, parsley, onion, celery leaves, and Worcestershire. Mix until well blended, then divide and form into eight oval patties (croquettes). 2. Coat a large nonstick lidded skillet with cooking spray; heat over medium heat until hot but not smoking. Sauté patties for 3 to 4 minutes on one side until golden brown, flip, and sauté the other side until golden. 3. Cover skillet, lower heat to low, and cook for 7 minutes. Make the Sauce: 4. While croquettes are cooking, in a small bowl, mix all sauce ingredients until combined well. Using a whisk, beat until light and creamy.

Per Serving

calories: 228 | fat: 9g | protein: 27g | carbs: 9g | fiber: 1g | sugar: 3g | sodium: 598mg

Southwest Salmon and Roasted Red Onion and Peppers

Prep time: 10 minutes | Cook time: 30 minutes | Serves 4

1 medium red bell pepper, sliced in strips
1 medium red onion, cut in ¼-inch slices
2 teaspoons chopped fresh cilantro
2 teaspoons garlic powder
1 teaspoon chili powder
¼ teaspoon salt
Dash freshly ground black pepper (optional)
1 pound (454 g) salmon fillet, cut into 4-ounce (113-g) pieces
1 tablespoon extra-virgin olive oil

1. Preheat the oven to 375ºF (190ºC). Line a baking sheet with parchment paper. 2. Place the peppers and onions on the prepared sheet pan and cover with foil. Bake the vegetables for about 15 minutes, but don't turn off the oven when this first timer goes off. 3. While the vegetables are cooking, in a small bowl, mix the cilantro, garlic powder, chili powder, salt, and pepper (if using). Coat the top of each piece of salmon with this mixture. 4. Open the oven when first timer goes off and add salmon pieces skin-side down on the baking sheet. Drizzle fish and veggies with oil. 5. Bake for another 12 to 15 minutes, until the fish flakes easily with a fork. Remove the pan and serve the salmon on top of the vegetables. 6. Store leftover vegetables in an airtight container in the refrigerator for up to 7 days and the salmon in a separate airtight container in the refrigerator for up to 3 days.

Per Serving

calories: 235 | fat: 13g | protein: 24g | carbs: 6g | fiber: 1g | sugar: 2g | sodium: 196mg

Tangy Swordfish and Tomatoes

Prep time: 10 minutes | Cook time: 9 minutes | Serves 4

Olive oil cooking spray
1 pound (454 g) swordfish steak
1½ cups chopped fresh tomatoes
2 teaspoons light soy sauce
1 tablespoon Dijon mustard
2½ teaspoons chopped fresh tarragon, or ¾ teaspoon dried
Salt and pepper, to taste

1. In a medium nonstick skillet, heat cooking spray over high heat until hot but not smoking; sear swordfish for 2 minutes on each side. 2. Lower heat to medium and pour tomatoes around fish. Drizzle fish with soy sauce, cover, and cook for 5 minutes. Remove fish from skillet and keep warm. 3. Add mustard and tarragon to tomatoes and stir well to combine. Add salt and pepper to taste.

Per Serving

calories: 159 | fat: 5g | protein: 23g | carbs: 6g | fiber: 1g | sugar: 2g | sodium: 188mg

Souvlaki-Style Swordfish

Prep time: 10 minutes | Cook time: 8 minutes | Serves 4

1 tablespoon fresh lemon juice
½ teaspoon dried oregano
½ teaspoon freshly ground black pepper
1 pound (454 g) skinless swordfish steaks
1 large cucumber, peeled, seeded, and grated
1 cup plain, fat-free yogurt
1½ teaspoons chopped fresh mint leaves
½ teaspoon chopped garlic
Olive oil cooking spray

1. Combine lemon juice, oregano, and pepper and sprinkle over fish. Cover and marinate in refrigerator for 15 minutes. 2. Wrap grated cucumber in a double layer of paper towels and squeeze to extract liquid. 3. Put cucumber, yogurt, mint, and garlic in a food processor and purée until smooth. 4. Preheat broiler and place rack in top position. Coat a nonstick broiler pan with cooking spray. Place fish on pan and broil, turning once, for about 4 minutes on each side, or until just cooked through.

Per Serving

calories: 198 | fat: 6g | protein: 25g | carbs: 12g | fiber: 1g | sugar: 4g | sodium: 216mg

Seared Tuna over Sesame Spinach

Prep time: 10 minutes | Cook time: 5 minutes | Serves 4

2 tablespoons low-sodium soy sauce
1 tablespoon fresh lime juice
½ teaspoon cayenne pepper
½ teaspoon salt

1 pound (454 g) fresh tuna (about 1 inch thick)
1 (16-ounce / 454-g) bag frozen chopped spinach
1 teaspoon sesame oil
1 tablespoon toasted sesame seeds (optional)

1. In a bowl or resealable plastic bag large enough to hold fish, combine soy sauce, lime juice, cayenne, and salt. 2. Add tuna, making sure that it's completely coated. Close bag or tightly cover bowl and marinate in refrigerator for 15 to 30 minutes. 3. While tuna is marinating, prepare spinach in microwave according to package directions. Toss with sesame oil and sesame seeds (if using). 4. Remove tuna from marinade and let excess drip off. 5. Heat a medium skillet over a medium-high heat. Sear tuna for 2 to 3 minutes on each side for medium rare, then slice into ½-inch-thick slices. Serve over spinach.

Per Serving
calories: 223 | fat: 8g | protein: 32g | carbs: 6g | fiber: 4g | sugar: 1g | sodium: 339mg

Crispy Baked Cod

Prep time: 10 minutes | Cook time: 10 minutes | Serves 6

Nonstick cooking spray
6 (4-ounce / 113-g) skinless cod fillets
¾ teaspoon salt
¼ teaspoon freshly ground black pepper
3 tablespoons extra-virgin olive oil, divided

Juice of 1 lemon, divided
¼ cup dried whole-wheat bread crumbs
3 tablespoons chopped fresh parsley
2 tablespoons chopped chives

1. Preheat the oven to 425°F (220°C). Coat a 9-by-13-inch baking dish with cooking spray. 2. Season the cod fillets on both sides with the salt and pepper and arrange in the baking dish so that they do not overlap each other. Drizzle the fish with 1½ tablespoons of olive oil and half the lemon juice. 3. In a small bowl, mix to combine the bread crumbs, parsley, and chives. Sprinkle the mixture over the fillets, and then drizzle them with the remaining 1½ tablespoons of olive oil and lemon juice. 4. Bake the fillets until the bread crumbs are crisp and the cod flakes easily with a fork, about 12 minutes, and serve.

Per Serving
calories: 165 | fat: 8g | protein: 18g | carbs: 5g | fiber: 0g | sugar: 1g | sodium: 411mg

Mahi-Mahi with Mango-Avocado Salsa

Prep time: 10 minutes | Cook time: 10 minutes | Serves 4

4 (4-ounce / 113-g) mahi-mahi fillets
2 tablespoons extra-virgin olive oil
1 tablespoon ground cumin
1 teaspoon chili powder
½ teaspoon onion powder
Salt

½ cup diced mango
¼ cup diced avocado
¼ cup finely chopped red onion
⅓ cup diced cherry tomatoes
2 tablespoons finely chopped fresh cilantro
2 tablespoons freshly squeezed lime juice
1 teaspoon minced jalapeño

1. Preheat the grill to medium heat. Set the mahi-mahi fillets on a plate, and drizzle with the olive oil. Rub to coat. 2. In a small bowl, mix together the cumin, chili powder, onion powder, and salt to taste. Rub the seasonings over each fillet. 3. In a small bowl, stir to combine the mango, avocado, onion, tomatoes, cilantro, lime juice, and jalapeño, and salt to taste. Refrigerate until serving. 4. Place the mahi-mahi on the grill. Cook for 3 to 4 minutes, then gently turn over and cook for 3 to 4 minutes longer, until the fish is opaque and flakes easily with a fork. 5. Serve the mahi-mahi with the salsa.

Per Serving
calories: 232 | fat: 10g | protein: 28g | carbs: 8g | fiber: 2g | sugar: 4g | sodium: 138mg

Mustard-Crusted Halibut

Prep time: 10 minutes | Cook time: 11 minutes | Serves 4

- 1 tablespoon Dijon mustard
- 1 tablespoon whole-grain mustard
- 1 teaspoon grated fresh lemon zest
- 1 teaspoon chopped fresh thyme, or ½ teaspoons dried
- 1 tablespoon light soy sauce
- 1 pound (454 g) halibut fillets, skinned
- ½ cup ground soy nuts
- 1 tablespoon chopped fresh parsley
- Olive oil cooking spray
- 1 garlic clove, minced
- 1 cup bottled clam juice
- Salt and pepper, to taste

1. In a shallow bowl, combine mustards, lemon zest, thyme, and soy sauce. Dip fish and turn to coat both sides, then remove fish. Reserve mustard mixture. 2. On a flat plate, mix ground soy nuts and parsley and dredge coated fillets in mixture, turning to coat both sides. 3. Coat a medium nonstick skillet with cooking spray and sauté fish over medium heat for 2 minutes on each side. Lower heat to low and cook fish for 3 more minutes, or until just cooked through. Remove fish from pan and keep warm. 4. Sauté garlic in pan for 1 minute, or until golden. Stir clam juice and reserved mustard mixture into pan, scraping up any browned bits, and simmer for 3 minutes until slightly reduced. Add salt and pepper to taste.

Per Serving

calories: 248 | fat: 9g | protein: 34g | carbs: 9g | fiber: 4g | sugar: 2g | sodium: 302mg

Crispy Baked Coconut Shrimp

Prep time: 15 minutes | Cook time: 15 minutes | Serves 4

- Nonstick cooking spray
- 1 cup unsweetened coconut flakes
- 2 teaspoons granulated onion
- 1 teaspoon garlic powder
- Salt
- Freshly ground black pepper
- 4 large egg whites, well beaten
- 1 pound (454 g) raw large shrimp, peeled and deveined

1. Preheat the oven to 400ºF (205ºC). Spray a baking sheet with cooking spray and set aside. 2. In a medium bowl, combine the coconut flakes, onion, garlic, salt, and pepper. Place the mixture on a large plate next to the egg whites. 3. Coat each shrimp in egg whites, then dredge in the coconut mixture and lay on the baking sheet. Bake for 10 to 15 minutes, until fully cooked and pink, turning once midway through. Serve hot.

Per Serving

calories: 263 | fat: 12g | protein: 33g | carbs: 7g | fiber: 2g | sugar: 1g | sodium: 654mg

Smoky Fish Frittata

Prep time: 10 minutes | Cook time: 5 minutes | Serves 1

- 2 eggs
- 3 tablespoons skim or low-fat milk
- Salt and freshly ground black pepper
- Low-fat cooking spray
- 2 ounces (57 g) hot smoked salmon or a small smoked fish fillet (peppered mackerel, kipper, or smoked trout), flaked or chopped
- 2 teaspoons snipped chives or 1 to 2 asparagus spears, cooked and chopped
- 1 teaspoon grated Parmesan cheese

1. Beat the eggs with the milk and salt and pepper until well-mixed. Preheat the broiler. 2. Generously spray a small nonstick omelet or sauté pan with low-fat cooking spray. Heat, add the egg mixture, and cook for 30 seconds. 3. Scatter over the flaked fish and chives or asparagus, and cook until the egg is almost set. 4. Sprinkle with the Parmesan cheese, place under the broiler, and cook until the cheese is golden. Serve at once, or allow to cool to serve.

Per Serving

calories: 240 | fat: 14g | protein: 27g | carbs: 2g | fiber: 0g | sugar: 1g | sodium: 415mg

Cajun-Spiced Catfish with Citrus-Horseradish Sauce

Prep time: 20 minutes | Cook time: 4 minutes | Serves 4

1 pound (454 g) skinless catfish fillets
2 teaspoons paprika
1 garlic clove, minced
1 teaspoon dried oregano
1 teaspoon dried thyme
½ teaspoon cayenne pepper
Olive oil cooking spray
Citrus-Horseradish Sauce:

¼ cup low-fat mayonnaise
¼ cup fat-free sour cream
½ teaspoon grated lemon zest
1½ teaspoons fresh lemon juice
½ teaspoon grated lime zest
1½ teaspoons fresh lime juice
1 teaspoon capers, drained
1 teaspoon prepared horseradish
¼ cup chopped fresh basil leaves

1. Place fish on flat plate. Combine paprika, garlic, oregano, thyme, and cayenne thoroughly and rub on fish. Cover with foil and refrigerate for 20 minutes. Make the Sauce: 2. While fish is chilling, combine all sauce ingredients in a medium bowl and whisk until smooth. 3. Preheat broiler and arrange rack to top position. Coat a nonstick broiling pan with cooking spray, place fish on it, and broil for 4 minutes, or until fish flakes easily with a fork. Serve with sauce.

Per Serving

calories: 160 | fat: 7g | protein: 24g | carbs: 4g | fiber: 1g | sugar: 2g | sodium: 165mg

Balinese Shrimp

Prep time: 10 minutes | Cook time: 12 minutes | Serves 4

Canola cooking spray
8 garlic cloves, minced
¾ cup water
1 teaspoon ground cumin
1 teaspoon ground coriander

½ teaspoon ground turmeric
1 pound (454 g) large shrimp, peeled and deveined
1 cup plain, fat-free yogurt
2 tablespoons dried chives
2 packets artificial sweetener (Splenda or Truvia)

1. In a large nonstick lidded skillet, heat cooking spray over medium heat until hot but not smoking. Add garlic and sauté until golden, about 30 seconds. 2. Stir in water, cumin, coriander, and turmeric; cover, lower heat, and simmer for 7 minutes. 3. Add shrimp and cook, uncovered, stirring, for 3 minutes, or until they turn pink. 4. Stir in yogurt, chives, and sweetener and simmer over very low heat for 2 minutes, stirring occasionally.

Per Serving

calories: 201 | fat: 3g | protein: 30g | carbs: 13g | fiber: 2g | sugar: 6g | sodium: 265mg

Zesty Lime Shrimp with Avocado

Prep time: 15 minutes | Cook time: 0 minutes | Serves 4

1 pound (454 g) cooked peeled and deveined shrimp
1 tomato, chopped
1 avocado, peeled, pitted, chopped, and tossed in a little lemon or lime juice
1 small jalapeño pepper, seeded and chopped
¼ red onion, finely chopped

Grated zest of 1 lime
Juice of 2 limes
1 teaspoon olive oil
1 tablespoon chopped fresh cilantro
Salt and freshly ground black pepper
Lime wedges, for serving (optional)

1. Mix the shrimp with the tomato, avocado, jalapeño, and red onion in a bowl. 2. Mix the lime zest with the lime juice, oil, cilantro, and salt and pepper, and pour over the shrimp mixture. Toss to mix well. 3. Serve with lime wedges for squeezing over, if desired.

Per Serving

calories: 189 | fat: 10g | protein: 17g | carbs: 10g | fiber: 4g | sugar: 2g | sodium: 549mg

Classic Crab-Stuffed Tomatoes

Prep time: 10 minutes | Cook time: 10 minutes | Serves 4

4 medium Roma tomatoes
1 cup lump crab meat or 1 (6-ounce / 170-g) can crab meat, drained
1 tablespoon olive oil mayonnaise
1 tablespoon low-fat plain Greek yogurt
1 tablespoon chopped fresh basil
1 teaspoon Dijon mustard
½ teaspoon freshly squeezed lemon juice
½ teaspoon hot sauce (optional)
2 tablespoons sliced scallions

1. Carefully cut off the top of each tomato, and scoop out the pulp and seeds from inside. Discard or save the pulp for use in soups, stews, and chili. 2. In a medium bowl, mix together the crab meat, mayonnaise, yogurt, basil, mustard, lemon juice, and hot sauce (if using). 3. Gently fill each tomato with the crab salad mixture, and top each with the chopped scallions. 4. Chill until ready to serve.

Per Serving (1 stuffed tomato)
calories: 94 | fat: 2g | protein: 10g | carbs: 9g | fiber: 2g | sugar: 4g | sodium: 229mg

Lemon-Parsley Crab Cakes

Prep time: 15 minutes | Cook time: 10 minutes | Serves 4

3 tablespoons whole-wheat bread crumbs
1 egg, lightly beaten
½ teaspoon Dijon mustard
1½ tablespoons olive oil-based mayonnaise
¼ teaspoon ground cayenne pepper
2 teaspoons chopped fresh parsley
Juice of ½ lemon
2 (6-ounce / 170-g) cans lump crab meat, drained and cartilage removed
Nonstick cooking spray

1. In a medium bowl, mix together the bread crumbs, egg, mustard, mayonnaise, cayenne pepper, parsley, and lemon juice. 2. Very gently fold in the lump crab meat. 3. Using a ¼-cup measuring cup, shape the mixture into 4 individual patties. Put the patties in the refrigerator and let sit for 30 minutes. 4. Preheat the oven to 500°F (260°C) while the crab cakes rest in the refrigerator. Coat a baking sheet with the cooking spray. 5. Place the crab cakes on the baking sheet and bake on the center rack of the oven 10 minutes, or until starting to brown. 6. Serve immediately.

Per Serving (1 crab cake)
calories: 148 | fat: 4g | protein: 21g | carbs: 5g | fiber: 0g | sugar: 1g | sodium: 464mg

Scallops Provençale

Prep time: 10 minutes | Cook time: 10 minutes | Serves 4

1 pound (454 g) large sea scallops, patted dry, tough side muscle removed (if necessary)
Olive oil cooking spray
4 garlic cloves, thinly sliced
1½ cups diced seeded fresh tomatoes
⅛ teaspoon dried thyme
¼ cup shredded fresh basil
½ cup dry white wine

1. Slice scallops in half horizontally. 2. In a nonstick skillet large enough to hold scallops in one layer, heat cooking spray over medium-high heat until it is hot but not smoking. Sear scallops for 1 to 2 minutes on each side, or until they are golden brown and just cooked through. Use a slotted spoon to transfer scallops to a platter and cover loosely to keep warm. 3. Re-spray pan and cook garlic over moderate heat, stirring until it is lightly browned. 4. Add tomatoes, thyme, and basil and cook, stirring, for 1 minute. 5. Add wine and cook, stirring, for 1 minute. Lower heat and simmer for about 5 minutes, or until tomatoes are soft and sauce is slightly thickened.

Per Serving
calories: 156 | fat: 2g | protein: 21g | carbs: 8g | fiber: 1g | sugar: 4g | sodium: 203mg

Scallops Piquant

Prep time: 10 minutes | Cook time: 10 minutes | Serves 4

Olive oil cooking spray
1 pound (454 g) sea scallops, patted dry, tough side muscle removed (if necessary)
½ cup minced shallots
½ cup white wine
½ cup water
¼ cup Dijon mustard

1. Heat cooking spray in a large nonstick skillet over medium-high heat until hot but not smoking. Sauté scallops for 1 to 2 minutes on each side (depending on size), or until golden and just cooked through. Remove from pan and keep warm. 2. Re-spray skillet and cook shallots over medium heat, stirring, for 1 minute until softened. 3. Add wine and boil, then cook, scraping up any browned bits, for 1 minute. Stir in water and mustard, lower heat, and simmer for 7 to 8 minutes, or until liquid is reduced to about ¾ cup.

Per Serving

calories: 154 | fat: 3g | protein: 20g | carbs: 10g | fiber: 1g | sugar: 6g | sodium: 251mg

Coquilles Saint-Jacques

Prep time: 10 minutes | Cook time: 10 minutes | Serves 4

Butter-flavored cooking spray
3 pinches crumbled saffron
1 pound (454 g) sea scallops, patted dry, tough side muscle removed (if necessary)
¼ cup minced shallots
1 tablespoon white wine
1 tablespoon dry vermouth
½ cup bottled clam juice
½ cup evaporated skim milk

1. Coat a large nonstick skillet with cooking spray. Sprinkle pan with a pinch of saffron and heat over medium-high heat until moderately hot but not smoking. 2. Add scallops in a single layer and cook them undisturbed for 2 minutes on each side, or until golden and just cooked through. Remove scallops and keep warm. 3. Re-spray pan, sprinkle with remaining saffron, and lower heat to low. Add shallots, stirring until soft. 4. Add wine and vermouth to deglaze skillet, scraping up any browned bits. Increase heat to medium-high, add clam juice, and boil until liquid is reduced by half. 5. Add evaporated milk and any scallop juices that have accumulated. Lower heat and simmer until reduced to a thickened, creamy consistency. Stir in scallops.

Per Serving

calories: 142 | fat: 1g | protein: 22g | carbs: 9g | fiber: 0g | sugar: 6g | sodium: 261mg

Chapter 13 Desserts

168 **Nutty Chocolate Bites** 87
169 **Mini Cheesecake Bites** 87
170 **Piña Colada Bark** 87
171 **Mocha Almond Bark** 88
172 **Peanut Butter and Jelly Coins** 88
173 **Zesty Clementine Cake** 88
174 **Maple-Sesame Peanuts** 89
175 **Chocolate Quinoa Crisps** 89
176 **Very Berry Mug Crumble** 89
177 **Chocolate Oatmeal Cookies** 90
178 **Grilled Stone Fruit with Greek Yogurt** 90
179 **Chocolate Brownies with Almond Butter** 90
180 **Chocolate-Dipped Apples with Coconut** 91
181 **Coconut Fruity Ice Pops** 91
182 **Apple and Blackberry Cake** 91
183 **Chocolate Protein Pudding Pops** 92
184 **Chocolate Chia Pudding** 92
185 **Lemon-Blackberry Frozen Yogurt** 92

Nutty Chocolate Bites

Prep time: 15 minutes | Cook time: 0 minutes | Serves 12

½ cup coconut oil, melted
¼ cup smooth natural peanut butter, melted
1 tablespoon butter, melted

2 tablespoons unsweetened cocoa powder, sifted
¼ cup chopped roasted peanuts

1. Line 12 wells of a mini muffin pan with paper liners and set aside. 2. In a small bowl, beat coconut oil, peanut butter and butter with an electric hand mixer until smooth and thoroughly combined. 3. Sprinkle cocoa powder over coconut oil mixture and continue beating until smooth and thoroughly combined. 4. Pour mixture into prepared pan and sprinkle with chopped peanuts. Place muffin pan in the freezer until cups are firm and chilled through, about 30 minutes. Serve and enjoy!

Per Serving
calories: 136 | fat: 14g | protein: 2g | carbs: 2g | fiber: 1g | sugar: 1g | sodium: 56mg

Mini Cheesecake Bites

Prep time: 10 minutes | Cook time: 30 minutes | Serves 6

1 tablespoon butter, melted
¼ cup almond flour
8 ounces (227 g) low-fat cream cheese, softened
2 tablespoons erythritol
1 large egg

1 teaspoon vanilla extract
1½ tablespoons low-fat sour cream
2 tablespoons freshly squeezed lemon juice
⅛ teaspoon salt
Fresh fruit, for serving (optional)

1. Preheat the oven to 325ºF (165ºC). 2. Line a 6-compartment muffin tin with muffin liners. 3. In a small bowl, combine the butter and almond flour until almost doughy. Divide the mixture evenly among the 6 muffin liners. Using your fingers, press the crust into an even layer. Bake for 10 minutes, remove from the oven, and set aside. 4. In a medium mixing bowl with a hand mixer, beat the cream cheese until fluffy. Add the erythritol slowly, and continue mixing. 5. Add the egg, vanilla, sour cream, lemon juice, and salt; beat until combined. 6. Pour 2 tablespoons of cheesecake mixture on top of each almond meal crust. Tap the muffin tin on the counter to bring any air bubbles to the top, then pop them. 7. Bake for 18 to 22 minutes, or until no longer jiggly. Remove from the oven and allow to cool for 15 minutes. Transfer to a wire rack to cool completely. Chill in the refrigerator for 2 to 4 hours or overnight. Serve topped with fresh fruit (if desired).

Per Serving
calories: 196 | fat: 19g | protein: 5g | carbs: 3g | fiber: 0g | sugar: 2g | sodium: 188mg

Piña Colada Bark

Prep time: 15 minutes | Cook time: 15 minutes | Serves 16

½ cup cocoa butter oil, melted
½ cup coconut oil, melted
Powdered sweetener of choice equal to 2 tablespoons sugar
1 tablespoon pineapple extract

1 teaspoon coconut extract
1 teaspoon rum extract
½ cup unsweetened shredded coconut, toasted

1. Line an 8-inch x 8-inch baking pan with aluminum foil and set aside. 2. In a medium bowl, mix cocoa butter, coconut oil, sweetener and extracts until thoroughly combined. 3. Pour mixture into prepared pan, spread evenly and sprinkle with coconut. Cover pan with plastic wrap and refrigerate until bark is chilled through and firm, about 1 hour. 4. Use foil to lift bark from pan. Cut bark into 16 squares and serve immediately. Enjoy!

Per Serving
calories: 137 | fat: 10g | protein: 0g | carbs: 2g | fiber: 0g | sugar: 0g | sodium: 48mg

Mocha Almond Bark

Prep time: 5 minutes | Cook time: 2 minutes | Serves 4

⅓ cup dark chocolate chips
½ teaspoon instant espresso powder

2 tablespoons slivered almonds
Pinch flaky salt (like Maldon)

1. Set aside a large piece of aluminum foil. 2. In a microwave-safe bowl, microwave the chocolate on high for 30 seconds, then remove and stir. Microwave again for 30 seconds and stir again. 3. Add the espresso powder, mix well, then microwave on high for another 30 seconds. 4. Using a rubber spatula, pour the melted chocolate onto the foil. Spread it out in a thin layer, about ¼ inch thick. 5. Sprinkle the slivered almonds and flaky salt on top. 6. Place the bark in the freezer to cool and harden for about 20 minutes, or until very hard and brittle. 7. Break the bark into smaller pieces and serve, or store in the freezer for up to 1 month.

Per Serving
calories: 112 | fat: 8g | protein: 1g | carbs: 13g | fiber: 2g | sugar: 9g | sodium: 45mg

Peanut Butter and Jelly Coins

Prep time: 10 minutes | Cook time: 2 minutes | Makes 8 coins

4 tablespoons dark chocolate chips or no-sugar-added chocolate

2 teaspoons peanut butter
8 raspberries

1. In a microwave-safe bowl, microwave the chocolate chips on high for 60 seconds, then remove and stir. Microwave again for 30 to 45 seconds, until the chocolate is fully melted. 2. On a piece of parchment paper, evenly drop the melted chocolate in small circular shapes, about 1 inch in diameter. 3. Top each with ¼ teaspoon peanut butter and freeze for at least 10 minutes or until the chocolate is firm and can be easily removed by gently peeling back the paper. 4. Top each chocolate coin with a single fresh raspberry and serve immediately.

Per Serving
calories: 43 | fat: 3g | protein: 1g | carbs: 5g | fiber: 1g | sugar: 4g | sodium: 9mg

Zesty Clementine Cake

Prep time: 10 minutes | Cook time: 2 hours | Serves 12

14 ounces (397 g) whole clementines, with skin
Low-fat cooking spray
Scant ½ cup honey
3 tablespoons olive oil

5 eggs
3 cups ground almonds or almond flour
1½ teaspoons baking powder

1. Place the clementines in a pan, and cover with water. Weight down with a smaller pan lid so that the clementines stay submerged in the water. Bring to a boil, lower the heat, and cook for 45 to 60 minutes, until they are very tender. Drain and let cool. When cool, cut in half and remove any seeds. 2. Preheat the oven to 350ºF (180ºC). Line the bottom of a 8½-inch springform pan with parchment paper and spray the sides with low-fat cooking spray. 3. Place the cooked clementines in a food processor and blend until smooth. 4. Add the honey, olive oil, and eggs, and pulse to combine. 5. Mix the ground almonds with the baking powder, add to the clementine mixture, and pulse until just mixed—do not overprocess. Pour the mixture into the prepared pan and bake for 50 minutes, or until the cake is well-risen, golden, firm to the touch, and a skewer inserted into the center of the cake comes out clean. Cover the top of the cake with foil or parchment paper if it starts to brown too much (check after 30 minutes). 6. Let cool in the pan, then turn out to serve, and cut into thin wedges. Decorate the top with a few slices of fresh clementine if serving on the same day. Use candied or dried clementine if storing for longer.

Per Serving
calories: 270 | fat: 20g | protein: 9g | carbs: 15g | fiber: 2g | sugar: 11g | sodium: 135mg

Maple-Sesame Peanuts

Prep time: 5 minutes | Cook time: 5 minutes | Makes about ½ cup

1 tablespoon maple syrup
½ cup roasted and salted shelled peanuts
2 teaspoons white sesame seeds
2 teaspoons black sesame seeds

1. In a medium nonstick skillet over medium heat, warm the maple syrup for about 30 seconds. 2. Add the peanuts and coat to combine, then turn off the heat and let the mixture sit for about 1 minute. 3. While the peanuts rest, in a small bowl, combine the sesame seeds. 4. Transfer the peanuts to a plate and sprinkle the sesame seeds on top. Let them cool and serve.

Per Serving (2 tablespoons)
calories: 138 | fat: 11g | protein: 5g | carbs: 8g | fiber: 2g | sugar: 4g | sodium: 151mg

Chocolate Quinoa Crisps

Prep time: 15 minutes | Cook time: 5 minutes | Makes 16 crisps

5 tablespoons coconut oil, melted, divided
1 cup dry quinoa
2 tablespoons maple syrup
2 tablespoons unsweetened cocoa powder
1 teaspoon vanilla extract
Sea salt

1. In a wide, heavy-bottomed saucepan (at least 6 inches deep with a lid) over medium heat, heat 1 tablespoon of coconut oil. 2. Add a few dried quinoa seeds. Once the pan is hot enough, the quinoa should pop. It will not expand as much as a popcorn kernel, but it will brown and jump in the air. 3. Cover the base of the pot with the remaining quinoa. 4. Gently shake the pot constantly to prevent sticking or burning of seeds. Remove from the heat once the popping starts to slow, usually after 1 to 5 minutes. Be sure not to let the quinoa burn. 5. Once the quinoa has stopped popping, pour onto a baking sheet to cool. 6. In a medium bowl, whisk together the remaining 4 tablespoons of coconut oil with the maple syrup, cocoa powder, and vanilla until smooth. Add salt to taste. 7. Fold in the puffed quinoa. 8. Scoop 1-tablespoon mounds of the mixture onto a lined baking sheet, and gently press to flatten. 9. Chill in the refrigerator or freezer for 30 to 60 minutes, until hardened. 10. Transfer to a large bag or airtight container, and keep refrigerated.

Per Serving
calories: 92 | fat: 5g | protein: 2g | carbs: 10g | fiber: 1g | sugar: 2g | sodium: 1mg

Very Berry Mug Crumble

Prep time: 10 minutes | Cook time: 3 minutes | Serves 1

About ½ cup mixed frozen berries or sliced autumn fruit
½ to 1 teaspoon brown sugar
¾ teaspoon cornstarch
Crumble:
3 tablespoons rolled oats
1½ teaspoons brown sugar
Pinch of ground cinnamon or ginger
1 teaspoon light butter or low-fat spread, melted

1. Place the frozen berries or autumn fruit in a small microwave-safe mug (about ¾ cup)—they should almost fill the mug. Sprinkle over the sugar to taste and the cornstarch. Microwave for 30 seconds. Stir gently, trying to keep the fruit whole, then microwave for an additional 25 seconds, or until the sauces from the fruit start to thicken. 2. Meanwhile, for the crumble, place the oats in a small cup or bowl and stir in the sugar, cinnamon or ginger, and butter or spread. Mix well, then spoon over the partially cooked fruit mixture. Place the mug inside a shallow bowl (since the mixture does have a tendency to bubble over) and microwave for 75 seconds. 3. Let stand for 1 minute before serving with a little low-fat custard, yogurt, or low-fat ice cream, if desired.

Per Serving
calories: 138 | fat: 4g | protein: 4g | carbs: 29g | fiber: 5g | sugar: 12g | sodium: 6mg

Chocolate Oatmeal Cookies

Prep time: 5 minutes | Cook time: 15 minutes | Makes 8 cookies

Nonstick cooking spray
2 medium ripe bananas
¾ cup old-fashioned rolled oats
1 tablespoon vanilla extract
1 tablespoon cocoa powder
2 tablespoons dark chocolate chips

1. Preheat the oven to 350ºF (180ºC). Line a baking sheet with aluminum foil and coat with cooking spray. 2. In a large bowl, using a large fork, mash together the bananas and oats. 3. Add the vanilla and cocoa powder to the banana mixture and combine. Fold the chocolate chips into the dough. 4. Using an ice scream scoop, scoop the dough into 2-inch balls and place on the prepared baking sheet. 5. Bake for 15 minutes, or until firm and golden brown on the bottom. 6. Serve warm or at room temperature, or freeze for up to 1 month.

Per Serving (2 cookies)
calories: 156 | fat: 4g | protein: 3g | carbs: 29g | fiber: 4g | sugar: 12g | sodium: 4mg

Grilled Stone Fruit with Greek Yogurt

Prep time: 5 minutes | Cook time: 5 minutes | Serves 6

Nonstick cooking spray
3 large fresh peaches, halved and pitted
1 teaspoon extra-virgin olive oil
6 ounces (170 g) low-fat, honey-flavored Greek yogurt
¼ cup sliced almonds
Ground cinnamon, for garnishing

1. Spray your grill (or a grill pan on the stovetop) with cooking spray. Heat the grill or grill pan to high heat, about 500ºF (260ºC). 2. Brush each peach half with olive oil. 3. Place the cut fruit on the grill flesh-side down, and grill for two minutes. Using tongs, turn the fruit over and cook for another 2 minutes. Transfer to a serving dish. 4. Serve the fruit with the Greek yogurt, and garnish with the almonds and cinnamon.

Per Serving
calories: 78 | fat: 3g | protein: 4g | carbs: 11g | fiber: 2g | sugar: 8g | sodium: 8mg

Chocolate Brownies with Almond Butter

Prep time: 5 minutes | Cook time: 25 minutes | Makes 16 brownies

Nonstick cooking spray
½ cup cocoa powder
1 tablespoon ground flaxseed
½ teaspoon ground instant coffee
¼ teaspoon baking soda
½ cup almond butter
¼ cup melted coconut oil
2 large eggs
1 teaspoon vanilla extract
½ cup agave nectar

1. Preheat the oven to 325ºF (165ºC). Coat an 8-by-8-inch glass baking dish with the cooking spray. 2. Place the cocoa powder, flaxseed, instant coffee, baking soda, almond butter, coconut oil, eggs, vanilla, and agave nectar in a high-speed blender or food processor. Blend on medium-high until smooth. Pour the batter into the baking dish. 3. Bake for 25 minutes or until a toothpick inserted in the middle comes out clean. Let cool for 10 minutes before cutting into 16 squares.

Per Serving (1 brownie)
calories: 124 | fat: 9g | protein: 3g | carbs: 11g | fiber: 2g | sugar: 9g | sodium: 49mg

Chocolate-Dipped Apples with Coconut

Prep time: 5 minutes | Cook time: 2 minutes | Serves 4

½ cup dark chocolate chips
¼ unsweetened shredded coconut
2 medium apples, cut into wedges

1. In a microwave-safe bowl, microwave the chocolate on high for 60 seconds, then remove and stir. Microwave again for 30 to 45 seconds, or until the chocolate is fully melted. 2. In a small bowl, place the coconut. Set the bowl next to a large plate. 3. Remove the chocolate from the microwave, stirring it once more. 4. Dip the bottom half of each apple slice into the melted chocolate. 5. Immediately dip the apple slice in the shredded coconut and place on the empty plate to set. 6. Let the chocolate harden, about 10 minutes, then serve.

Per Serving
calories: 201 | fat: 12g | protein: 0g | carbs: 29g | fiber: 4g | sugar: 21g | sodium: 11mg

Coconut Fruity Ice Pops

Prep time: 10 minutes | Cook time: 0 minutes | Serves 8

2½ cups unsweetened coconut water
1¼ pounds (567 g) cubed or sliced soft fruit (such as strawberries, mango, kiwi, or raspberries)
2 to 3 tablespoons agave nectar or your favorite sweetener

1. Place the coconut water and half of your chosen fruit in a blender, and blend until smooth. Add the agave nectar and blend again, adjusting the sweetness to taste (remember, sweetness diminishes with freezing). 2. Divide the remaining fruit among popsicle molds (about 8) then top with the puréed fruit mixture. 3. Freeze for at least 4 hours, or overnight, until solid. 4. To remove the popsicles from the molds easily, try plunging them briefly in warm water to tease them out.

Per Serving
calories: 40 | fat: 0g | protein: 1g | carbs: 10g | fiber: 1g | sugar: 7g | sodium: 15mg

Apple and Blackberry Cake

Prep time: 20 minutes | Cook time: 40 minutes | Serves 8

1 cup all-purpose flour
1 heaping tablespoon granulated sweetener
2 teaspoons finely grated lemon zest
2 teaspoons baking powder
3 eggs
3 tablespoons low-fat milk
3 ounces (85 g) low-fat spread or light butter, melted
2 pounds (907 g) assorted apples, peeled, cored, and cut into slices
Low-fat cooking spray
½ cup blackberries
2 tablespoons sliced almonds
Sifted confectioners' sugar, to decorate (optional)

1. Preheat the oven to 400°F (205°C)). 2. In a large bowl, mix the flour with the sweetener, lemon zest, and baking powder. Make a well in the center and add the eggs and milk. Whisk, then add the melted spread or light butter and mix well. 3. Add the apple slices to the batter and fold in lightly. 4. Spray a 9-inch nonstick springform pan with low-fat cooking spray. Add the batter and sprinkle with the blackberries and sliced almonds. Bake for 30 to 40 minutes, until well-risen, firm, and golden. 5. Allow to cool slightly before serving, dusted with confectioners' sugar, if desired. Cut into slices to serve.

Per Serving
calories: 175 | fat: 7g | protein: 6g | carbs: 21g | fiber: 4g | sugar: 15g | sodium: 268mg

Chocolate Protein Pudding Pops

Prep time: 5 minutes | Cook time: 0 minutes | Serves 4

1 (3.9-ounce / 111-g) package chocolate-flavored instant pudding

2 cups cold low-fat milk
2 scoops chocolate protein powder

1. In a medium bowl, whisk the pudding mix, milk, and protein powder for at least 2 minutes. 2. Spoon into ice pop molds or paper cups. Insert an ice pop stick into the center of each mold or cup. 3. Freeze for 4 hours, or until firm. Remove from the molds or cups before serving.

Per Serving
calories: 215 | fat: 2g | protein: 12g | carbs: 36g | fiber: 0g | sugar: 25g | sodium: 102mg

Chocolate Chia Pudding

Prep time: 15 minutes | Cook time: 0 minutes | Serves 4

2 cups unsweetened soy milk
10 drops liquid stevia
¼ cup unsweetened cocoa powder
¼ teaspoon ground cinnamon

¼ teaspoon vanilla extract
½ cup chia seeds
½ cup fresh raspberries, for garnish

1. In a small bowl, whisk together the soy milk, stevia, cocoa powder, cinnamon, and vanilla until well combined. 2. Stir in the chia seeds. 3. Divide between 4 small serving dishes. 4. Cover and refrigerate for at least 1 hour, or overnight. 5. When ready to serve, garnish with the raspberries.

Per Serving (½ cup)
calories: 182 | fat: 9g | protein: 11g | carbs: 16g | fiber: 14g | sugar: 1g | sodium: 36mg

Lemon-Blackberry Frozen Yogurt

Prep time: 5 minutes | Cook time: 0 minutes | Makes 4 cups

4 cups frozen blackberries
½ cup low-fat plain Greek yogurt
Juice of 1 lemon

2 teaspoons liquid stevia
Fresh mint leaves, for garnish

1. In a blender or food processor, add the blackberries, yogurt, lemon juice, and stevia. Blend until smooth, about 5 minutes. 2. Serve immediately or freeze in an airtight container and use within 3 weeks. Garnish with fresh mint leaves.

Per Serving (⅔ cup)
calories: 68 | fat: 0g | protein: 3g | carbs: 15g | fiber: 5g | sugar: 11g | sodium: 12mg

Chapter 14 Staples, Sauces and Dressings

186 **Vegan Spinach Pesto**   94
187 **Black Bean Hummus**   94
188 **Greek Yogurt Onion Dip**   94
189 **Lightened-Up Blue Cheese Dip**   94
190 **Garlic Sauce**   95
191 **Papaya Sauce**   95
192 **Stir-Fry Sauce**   95
193 **Tzatziki Sauce**   95
194 **Creamy Peppercorn Ranch Dressing**   96
195 **Spicy Peanut Dressing**   96
196 **Greek Yogurt Caesar Dressing**   96
197 **Citrus-Avocado Salad Dressing**   96
198 **Homemade Condensed Cream of Mushroom Soup**   97
199 **Balsamic Vinaigrette**   97
200 **Egg Custard Sauce**   97
201 **Fresh Salsa**   98
202 **Creamy Peanut Sauce**   98
203 **Taco seasoning**   98

Vegan Spinach Pesto

Prep time: 5 minutes | Cook time: 0 minutes | Makes about ¾ cup

1 (10-ounce / 283-g) bag baby spinach
¼ cup extra-virgin olive oil
Juice of 2 lemons
¼ cup roasted salted cashews
2 garlic cloves, peeled
Salt

1. In a food processor or blender, combine the spinach, olive oil, and lemon juice and blend until the spinach is well chopped. 2. Add the cashews and garlic and continue to blend until well incorporated. 3. Season with salt and serve. To store, refrigerate in an airtight container for up to 1 week.

Per Serving (3 tablespoons)
calories: 194 | fat: 18g | protein: 3g | carbs: 8g | fiber: 2g | sugar: 1g | sodium: 109mg

Black Bean Hummus

Prep time: 5 minutes | Cook time: 0 minutes | Makes about 1½ cup

1 (15½-ounce / 439-g) can black beans, rinsed and drained
2 tablespoons tahini
1 tablespoon toasted sesame oil
Juice of 2 limes
2 garlic cloves, peeled
Salt

1. In a blender or food processor, pulse the black beans until they are chopped into smaller pieces. 2. Add the tahini, sesame oil, lime juice, and garlic, then blend for about 2 minutes, until very smooth. 3. If the hummus is too thick for your liking, add water 1 teaspoon at a time. 4. Season with salt and serve. To store, refrigerate in an airtight container for up to 1 week.

Per Serving (¼ cup)
calories: 119 | fat: 5g | protein: 5g | carbs: 13g | fiber: 4g | sugar: 1g | sodium: 6mg

Greek Yogurt Onion Dip

Prep time: 5 minutes | Cook time: 0 minutes | Makes about 1 cup

1 cup plain nonfat Greek yogurt
1 (28-gram) packet dried onion soup mix
Freshly ground black pepper

1. In a small bowl, combine the Greek yogurt with the onion soup mix and whisk well to combine. 2. Season with black pepper. Serve immediately or cover and refrigerate to serve cold. To store, refrigerate in an airtight container for up to 1 week.

Per Serving (¼ cup)
calories: 53 | fat: 0g | protein: 6g | carbs: 7g | fiber: 0g | sugar: 3g | sodium: 636mg

Lightened-Up Blue Cheese Dip

Prep time: 5 minutes | Cook time: 0 minutes | Makes about 1½ cup

1 cup plain nonfat Greek yogurt
3 tablespoons crumbled blue cheese
Juice of 1 lemon
1 teaspoon garlic powder
Salt
Freshly ground black pepper

1. In a medium bowl, combine the yogurt and blue cheese and stir well. 2. Add the lemon juice and garlic powder and stir again. Season with salt and pepper. 3. Serve immediately as a dip for vegetables or with your favorite protein. To store, refrigerate in an airtight container for up to 1 week.

Per Serving (⅓ cup)
calories: 63 | fat: 2g | protein: 7g | carbs: 4g | fiber: 0g | sugar: 3g | sodium: 115mg

Garlic Sauce

Prep time: 5 minutes | Cook time: 0 minutes | Makes approximately 1 cup

½ cup plain, fat-free yogurt
4 garlic cloves, finely minced

1 tablespoon fresh lemon juice
½ cup low-sodium chicken broth

1. Pour yogurt into a fine-mesh strainer over a small bowl and let stand for 15 minutes. Discard any liquid that has drained from yogurt. 2. In a small bowl, crush garlic until it forms a paste, then stir in lemon juice. 3. Add drained yogurt to garlic mixture and stir well. 4. In a small saucepan, bring chicken broth to a simmer, stir in yogurt-garlic mixture, and simmer for 1 minute more, stirring constantly.

Per Serving (2 tablespoons)
calories: 14 | fat: 0g | protein: 1g | carbs: 2g | fiber: 0g | sugar: 1g | sodium: 17mg

Papaya Sauce

Prep time: 5 minutes | Cook time: 0 minutes | Makes approximately 1 cup

½ large very ripe papaya (about 1 cup)
¼ teaspoon vanilla extract

1 tablespoon fresh lime juice
Artificial sweetener (Splenda or Truvia) to taste (optional)

1. Peel and seed papaya and scoop flesh into a food processor or blender. 2. Add vanilla and lime juice and purée until very smooth (if sauce is not sweet enough, add artificial sweetener to taste).

Per Serving (2 tablespoons)
calories: 9 | fat: 0g | protein: 0g | carbs: 3g | fiber: 0g | sugar: 1g | sodium: 0mg

Stir-Fry Sauce

Prep time: 5 minutes | Cook time: 0 minutes | Makes about ¾ cup

¼ cup low-sodium soy sauce
1 tablespoon freshly grated ginger
2 garlic cloves, minced

2 tablespoons brown sugar (or sugar substitute)
¼ cup water
1 teaspoon sriracha
2 tablespoons rice vinegar

1. In a medium bowl, whisk to combine the soy sauce, ginger, garlic, sugar, water, sriracha, and vinegar. 2. Refrigerate in an airtight container for up to one week.

Per Serving (¼ cup)
calories: 42 | fat: 0g | protein: 1g | carbs: 11g | fiber: 0g | sugar: 6g | sodium: 503mg

Tzatziki Sauce

Prep time: 10 minutes | Cook time: 0 minutes | Makes about 2 cups

1 cup shredded cucumber, seeded and grated
1 cup low-fat, plain Greek yogurt
1 tablespoon extra-virgin olive oil
1 tablespoon fresh dill

1 tablespoon freshly squeezed lemon juice
1 garlic clove, minced
Salt
Freshly ground black pepper

1. Using paper towels, pat dry the cucumber shreds, removing as much liquid as you can. 2. In a large bowl, mix the cucumber, yogurt, olive oil, dill, lemon juice, garlic, and salt and pepper to taste. 3. Serve immediately, or refrigerate in an airtight container for up to 5 days.

Per Serving (¼ cup)
calories: 40 | fat: 2g | protein: 3g | carbs: 2g | fiber: 0g | sugar: 1g | sodium: 18mg

Creamy Peppercorn Ranch Dressing

Prep time: 10 minutes | Cook time: 0 minutes | Makes 1 cup

¾ cup low-fat plain Greek yogurt
⅓ cup grated Parmigiano-Reggiano cheese
¼ cup low-fat buttermilk

Juice of 1 lemon
2 teaspoons freshly ground black pepper
½ teaspoon onion flakes
¼ teaspoon salt

1. In a blender or food processor, purée the yogurt, cheese, buttermilk, lemon juice, pepper, onion flakes, and salt on medium-high speed until the dressing is completely smooth and creamy.

Per Serving (2 tablespoons)
calories: 35 | fat: 1g | protein: 4g | carbs: 2g | fiber: 0g | sugar: 1g | sodium: 133mg

Spicy Peanut Dressing

Prep time: 5 minutes | Cook time: 0 minutes | Makes about ⅔ cup

¼ cup powdered peanut butter
2 tablespoons water
2 tablespoons rice vinegar
2 tablespoons low-sodium soy sauce

1 teaspoon sesame oil
1 teaspoon fresh ginger, minced
½ teaspoon sriracha (optional)
½ teaspoon fish sauce (optional)

1. In a medium bowl, whisk the powdered peanut butter, water, vinegar, soy sauce, sesame oil, ginger, sriracha, and fish sauce until well combined. 2. Refrigerate in an airtight jar for up to one week.

Per Serving (⅓ cup)
calories: 76 | fat: 4g | protein: 6g | carbs: 6g | fiber: 2g | sugar: 1g | sodium: 566mg

Greek Yogurt Caesar Dressing

Prep time: 5 minutes | Cook time: 0 minutes | Makes ½ cup

½ cup nonfat plain Greek yogurt
½ cup shredded Parmesan cheese
Juice of 1 small lemon (2 tablespoons)
1 tablespoon extra-virgin olive oil

1 teaspoon garlic powder
¼ teaspoon salt
Dash freshly ground black pepper

1. Add the yogurt, Parmesan cheese, lemon juice, oil, garlic powder, salt, and pepper to a blender. 2. Blend on low for about 30 seconds or until smooth. 3. Store the dressing in an airtight container in the refrigerator for up to 7 days for maximum freshness.

Per Serving (2 tablespoons)
calories: 100 | fat: 7g | protein: 7g | carbs: 3g | fiber: 0g | sugar: 1g | sodium: 382mg

Citrus-Avocado Salad Dressing

Prep time: 5 minutes | Cook time: 0 minutes | Makes 1 cup

¾ cup nonfat plain Greek yogurt
½ cup mashed avocado (½ avocado)
1 tablespoon freshly squeezed lemon juice

1 teaspoon dried or chopped fresh cilantro
1 teaspoon garlic powder
¼ teaspoon salt

1. In a medium mixing bowl, combine the yogurt, avocado, lemon juice, cilantro, garlic powder, and salt and mix well. 2. If you prefer a creamier, smoother texture, place all the ingredients into a blender and blend for about 1 minute on low. 3. Store in an airtight container in the refrigerator for up to 3 days.

Per Serving (3 tablespoons)
calories: 71 | fat: 4g | protein: 5g | carbs: 4g | fiber: 1g | sugar: 1g | sodium: 164mg

Homemade Condensed Cream of Mushroom Soup

Prep time: 10 minutes | Cook time: 10 minutes | Makes 1 (10¾-ounce / 305-g) can

4 teaspoons extra-virgin olive oil, divided
4 ounces (113 g) mushrooms
2 tablespoons whole-wheat pastry flour
½ cup vegetable or chicken broth
½ cup low-fat milk
½ teaspoon freshly ground black pepper

1. In a medium skillet over medium heat, heat 1 teaspoon of olive oil. Add the mushrooms, and sauté until tender, about 5 minutes. Remove the skillet and set aside. 2. In a medium saucepan over medium heat, heat the remaining 3 teaspoons of olive oil. 3. Gradually add the flour, and stir constantly until it is blended with the oil and the mixture is smooth. Turn off the heat. 4. Slowly add the broth and milk, whisking constantly until the mixture is smooth. 5. Stir in the mushrooms, and bring the mixture to a boil over medium-high heat. Stir in the pepper, reduce the heat to low, and simmer for 5 minutes. 6. Use as a substitute for 1 (10¾-ounce / 305-g) can of condensed cream of mushroom soup in recipes.

Per Serving (⅛ cup)

calories: 39 | fat: 3g | protein: 1g | carbs: 3g | fiber: 0g | sugar: 0g | sodium: 41mg

Balsamic Vinaigrette

Prep time: 5 minutes | Cook time: 0 minutes | Makes about ½ cup

2 tablespoons Dijon mustard
2 tablespoons balsamic vinegar
2 tablespoons honey
2 tablespoons extra-virgin olive oil
Salt
Freshly ground black pepper

1. In a medium bowl, whisk the Dijon and balsamic vinegar together until well combined. 2. Add the honey and whisk well. 3. Slowly drizzle the olive oil into the vinegar mixture and whisk until well combined. 4. Season with salt and pepper. Serve, or store in an airtight container in the refrigerator for up to 5 days.

Per Serving (2 tablespoons)

calories: 103 | fat: 7g | protein: 0g | carbs: 10g | fiber: 0g | sugar: 9g | sodium: 183mg

Egg Custard Sauce

Prep time: 5 minutes | Cook time: 5 minutes | Serves 4

2½ cups semi-skim or low-fat milk
4 large egg yolks
¼ cup granulated sweetener
½ teaspoon vanilla extract

1. Pour the milk into a heavy pan and bring slowly to a boil. 2. In a large bowl, whisk the egg yolks with the sweetener and vanilla, until creamy. 3. Slowly pour the hot milk into the egg yolk mixture and whisk well to blend. Rinse out the saucepan. 4. Strain the mixture through a sieve back into the pan and place over low heat. Cook, stirring constantly, until the custard thickens enough to coat the back of a spoon and has the consistency of thick cream. 5. Serve plain, warm or cold, dusted with grated nutmeg, if desired, or with slices of banana or puréed fruit.

Per Serving

calories: 132 | fat: 7g | protein: 8g | carbs: 9g | fiber: 2g | sugar: 6g | sodium: 201mg

Fresh Salsa

Prep time: 15 minutes | Cook time: 0 minutes | Makes 2 cups

3 medium tomatoes, diced
⅓ cup chopped green bell pepper
¼ cup chopped onion
¼ cup chopped scallions
1 teaspoon apple cider vinegar
1 teaspoon freshly squeezed lemon juice
1 teaspoon extra-virgin olive oil
1 teaspoon minced jalapeño pepper
1 teaspoon ground cumin
¼ teaspoon salt
¼ teaspoon ground cayenne pepper
¼ cup fresh chopped fresh cilantro

1. In a medium bowl, mix together the tomatoes, bell pepper, onion, scallions, vinegar, lemon juice, olive oil, jalapeño, cumin, salt, cayenne pepper, and cilantro. Enjoy immediately, or refrigerate for up to 3 days.

Per Serving (¼ cup)
calories: 16 | fat: 0g | protein: 1g | carbs: 3g | fiber: 1g | sugar: 2g | sodium: 76mg

Creamy Peanut Sauce

Prep time: 5 minutes | Cook time: 0 minutes | Makes ¾ cup

⅔ cup cubed firm tofu
2 tablespoons unsweetened peanut butter
2 tablespoons coconut aminos
1 teaspoon garlic powder
1 teaspoon ginger powder
1 teaspoon freshly squeezed lime juice
½ teaspoon chili garlic sauce
¼ teaspoon salt

1. Add the tofu, peanut butter, coconut aminos, garlic powder, ginger powder, lime juice, chili garlic sauce, and salt to a blender. 2. Blend on low for about 30 to 60 seconds or until smooth. 3. Store in an airtight container for up to 7 days for the best freshness.

Per Serving (3 tablespoons)
calories: 92 | fat: 6g | protein: 5g | carbs: 5g | fiber: 2g | sugar: 2g | sodium: 309mg

Taco seasoning

Prep time: 5 minutes | Cook time: 0 minutes | Makes about ½ cup

2 tablespoons chili powder
3 teaspoons ground cumin
1 teaspoon garlic powder
½ teaspoon onion powder
1 teaspoon dried oregano
2 teaspoons ground paprika
½ teaspoon salt
½ teaspoon freshly ground black pepper

1. In a resealable container, combine the chili powder, cumin, garlic powder, onion powder, oregano, paprika, salt, and pepper, and mix well. 2. Store in an airtight container for up to 3 months.

Per Serving (2 tablespoons)
calories: 26 | fat: 1g | protein: 1g | carbs: 4g | fiber: 2g | sugar: 0g | sodium: 229mg

Appendix 1 Measurement Conversion Chart

VOLUME EQUIVALENTS(DRY)

US STANDARD	METRIC (APPROXIMATE)
1/8 teaspoon	0.5 mL
1/4 teaspoon	1 mL
1/2 teaspoon	2 mL
3/4 teaspoon	4 mL
1 teaspoon	5 mL
1 tablespoon	15 mL
1/4 cup	59 mL
1/2 cup	118 mL
3/4 cup	177 mL
1 cup	235 mL
2 cups	475 mL
3 cups	700 mL
4 cups	1 L

VOLUME EQUIVALENTS(LIQUID)

US STANDARD	US STANDARD (OUNCES)	METRIC (APPROXIMATE)
2 tablespoons	1 fl.oz.	30 mL
1/4 cup	2 fl.oz.	60 mL
1/2 cup	4 fl.oz.	120 mL
1 cup	8 fl.oz.	240 mL
1 1/2 cup	12 fl.oz.	355 mL
2 cups or 1 pint	16 fl.oz.	475 mL
4 cups or 1 quart	32 fl.oz.	1 L
1 gallon	128 fl.oz.	4 L

TEMPERATURES EQUIVALENTS

FAHRENHEIT(F)	CELSIUS(C) (APPROXIMATE)
225 °F	107 °C
250 °F	120 °C
275 °F	135 °C
300 °F	150 °C
325 °F	160 °C
350 °F	180 °C
375 °F	190 °C
400 °F	205 °C
425 °F	220 °C
450 °F	235 °C
475 °F	245 °C
500 °F	260 °C

WEIGHT EQUIVALENTS

US STANDARD	METRIC (APPROXIMATE)
1 ounce	28 g
2 ounces	57 g
5 ounces	142 g
10 ounces	284 g
15 ounces	425 g
16 ounces (1 pound)	455 g
1.5 pounds	680 g
2 pounds	907 g

Printed in Great Britain
by Amazon